"If, like me, you are not familiar with the uniqueness of Appalachian culture and more specifically, the 'Affrilachian' experience, look no further. You don't need to spend one dime on gas. Just open the cover on this book and walk right in through Lyn Ford's wide open door. Before you even get to the tales, she tickles our senses with family reminiscences of asaphoetida bags, sassafras tea, chow-chow, northern gumbo, catfish and "licking homemade ice-cream from the dasher in the ice-cream churn"; a time when "nothing was wasted and everything tasted good". Then, written as she both remembers and performs them, Lyn serves us familiar tales with an Affilachian spin that feel fresh and new to the ear and the heart. Each family reminiscence; each handed down tale left me either lickin' my lips or splittin' my sides. When I closed the book, I felt like I'd just been given a party--a party that said welcome home friend."

**– Charlotte Blake Alston, Storyteller for the
Philadelphia Symphony Orchestra,
Independent Touring Storyteller and Teacher,
Philadelphia, PA**

"Lyn's stories bring her native world—the Appalachian culture of African-Americans--to life with wonder, laughter and wisdom."

**– Judy Sima, Storyteller, Author, Teaching Artist,
Former North Central Regional Director
of the National Storytelling Network.**

T0094866

"Lyn Ford has gathered a broad range of stories: trickster tales and pourquoi tales for young listeners as well as Jack tales, fool tales, wisdom tales, and ghost stories for adolescents and adults. Her notes and narrative affectionately reveal the traditions and values of a culture that is new to many of us. Bravo!"

– Mary Grace Ketner, Storyteller, Austin, TX

"In this collection Lyn Ford's guides readers on a journey through a rich and unique landscape peopled with characters and plots as unusual as they are delightful."

–Jim May, Storyteller, Author and Educator, Illinois

Affrilachian Tales

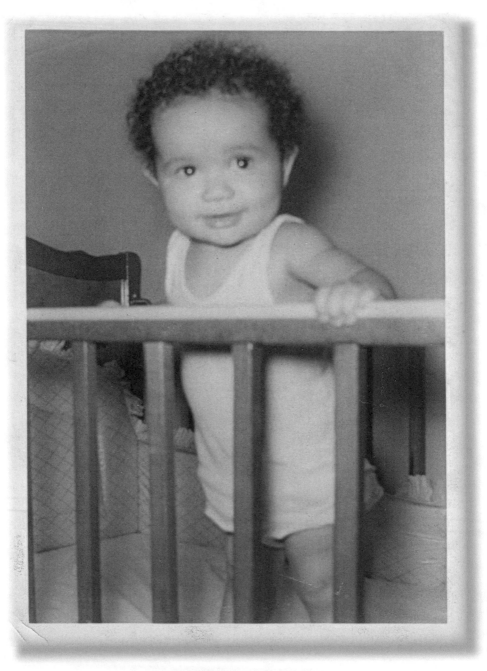

The author at 11months

Affrilachian Tales

FOLKTALES FROM THE AFRICAN-AMERICAN APPALACHIAN TRADITION

RETOLD BY
LYN FORD

PARKHURST BROTHERS, INC., PUBLISHERS

Little Rock, Arkansas

www.parkhurstbrothers.com

Parkhurst Brothers books are distributed to the trade through the Chicago Distribution Center, and may be ordered through Ingram Book Company, Baker & Taylor, Follett Library Resources and other book industry wholesalers. To order from Chicago's Chicago Distribution Center, phone 1-800-621-2736 or send a fax to 800-621-8476. Copies of this and other Parkhurst Brothers Inc., Publishers titles are available to organizations and corporations for purchase in quantity by contacting Special Sales Department at our home office location, listed on our web site. Manuscript submission guidelines for this publishing company are available at our web site.

Printed in the United States of America

First Edition, 2012

2012 2013 2014 2015 2016 2017   12 11 10 9 8 7 6 5 4 3 2 1

 Library of Congress Cataloging in Publication Data:
Ford, Lyn, 1951-
 Affrilachian tales : folktales from the African-American Appalachian tradition / retold by Lyn Ford.
    p. cm.
 ISBN 978-1-935166-65-8 (alk. paper) -- ISBN 978-1-935166-64-1
 1. African Americans--Appalachian Region--Folklore. 2. Tales--Appalachian Region. I. Title.
 GR111.A47F67 2012
 398.20974--dc23

                              2012012420

ISBN: Trade Paperback   978-1-935166-66-5   [10 digit: 1-935166-66-2]
ISBN: e-book   978-1-935166-67-2   [10-digit: 1-935166-67-0]

This book is printed on archival-quality paper that meets requirements of the American National Standard for Information Sciences, Permanence of Paper, Printed Library Materials, ANSI Z39.48-1984.

Cover and page design: Charlie Ross
Acquired for Parkhurst Brothers Inc., Publishers by: Ted Parkhurst
Editor: Barbara Paddack

102012   VPI

"AFFRILACHIAN"* (af.ruh.LAY.shun) adj. Relating to an
African-American who lives in Appalachia.
Also: Afrilachian. —Afrilachia n.

*Paul McFedries at Wordspy,
http://www.wordspy.com/words/affrilachian.asp

My father, Edward Maclin Cooper

Dedicated, with love, to:

My family, with whom my stories began;

My husband, Bruce, and our children—you have always believed in me, and never denied me the chance to be who I am.

Ted Parkhurst, my publisher and friend, and the giver of the go-for-it gumption I needed to get this on paper;

The grand folks of Affrilachian storytelling who blessed, inspired, and supported me, especially Mother Mary Carter Smith, born in Birmingham in Jefferson County, Alabama;

Mother Mary now shares stories with the ancestors.

Mama Linda Goss, born in Alcoa in Blount County, Tennessee;

Mother Mary and Mama Linda had the foresight and fortitude to imagine and create the National Association of Black Storytellers.

Table of Contents

Have you ever seen a briar patch? It is a thicket of
thorny branches. Folks who live in the hills may call it a
bramble or blackberry patch. The briar patch is a tangle
where the thorns are sharp, and the berries are sweet.
Rabbit was born and raised in the briar patch, a
metaphor for being born into troubles. But wise and
tricky Rabbit knows about troubles; he knows how
to avoid them, and how to use them as shelter and
protection from the bullies of the forest. Rabbit knows
how to survive in troubles, get out of troubles, or
simply leave them alone. The rewards for having such
wisdom are as sweet as blackberries.

Folktales gave me lessons for the thorny patches
of life. But when I was a child, I didn't know I was
learning something. I just knew the stories were as
sweet as blackberries.

I heard fables and pourquoi ("how" or "why") tales
from the first moments of storytelling that I can
remember. I know these were the purview of my
dad and my grandfather more than anyone else. At

bedtime, Ma read Aesop's fables to us, and Rudyard Kipling's animal stories; she gave each story depth and wonder through the music and power of her voice. But the fables attributed to Aesop hold very little characterization, very little back story on their protagonist and antagonists. They are wonderful anecdotes, but as a child drawn to the spoken word, I wanted more.

"More" was a possum who could sing, a rabbit who could sit on a front porch or fall in love, a heckling bull frog, a snake who wore a coat of many colors. The polished facets of told stories outshone the polished morality of the fabulous stories in books. I could understand and appreciate the story of "Hare and Tortoise", but I could "see" the story of "Possum and Snake" as if it were a movie in my head.

Now, here I am, putting those spoken-word treasures in a book! Ma is pleased and proud. Daddy is laughing and shaking his head in Heaven.

Our family's folktales are largely populated with critters of the four-legged, winged, and occasionally finned variety, but a small number of two-legged folks walk along the paths of a few tales. Some of them have names like John or Sarah Mae, but some are nameless—"that girl," "a young man," "an old man and an old woman;" their genealogy can be traced to the British Isles, to the hero of the beanstalk story and the fool tales in which someone who was called "clever" probably wasn't. A few stories of these women and men, or their children and grandchildren, remain in my memory and come to life in my storytelling.

Some of my favorite tales were the kind that might
keep me up at night. They were sometimes silly, and
sometimes frightening, but always awe-inspiring. The
term "haint" is apparently a regional one. From my own
travels and conversations, I have found that the word
is spoken and understood by folks from West Virginia
to Florida, and in the states along the Gulf of Mexico
through Texas. When I use it just about anywhere else,
somebody asks, "Do you mean 'haunt'?" Of course this
"thang" is a "haunt", a lost and drifting spirit or soul.
But most haints are angry, or vengeful, or at least a
bit mischievous and ornery. They live in cabins in the
woods, or old houses on hills or in swampy valleys,
nothing as fine as a mansion, unless it's been abandoned
and left to fall into ruin. "Haunt" is just too proper a word
for them.

    "Spookers" are creatures in the shadows, but they're
not necessarily dead. They are the thing you might see
from the corner of your eye, the dead thing revived
and walking or sitting where it might torment you, the
monster that creeps up the stairs or waits at the foot
of the bed. They are thangs, haints, boo hags, big boo
daddies, little boo babies, monsters, ghosts . . . there were
so many of these creatures in my daddy's stories that I
grew up unafraid of such things, because I knew them.

I'd already met them in stories. As my great-grandmother, Essie Arkward, said, "Dead folks don't bother you much. It's the living folks you have to worry about."

NOTE: Each story is followed by a brief note in which I discuss my connections to the story, as well as a few sources of variants.

Preface

After completing a program for a family-audience event, at a place in the designated-Appalachian region of Southern Ohio, where the audience appeared to be entirely of one culture, and where I had introduced myself as an Affrilachian and explained the meaning of that word, I was introduced to a local folklorist, who will remain appropriately unnamed. The gentleman said, "You shouldn't use that word, what did you say, 'Affrilachian?' I'm a folklorist, and the local storyteller. And I've never heard that word before; it is not a recognized description of any Appalachian people. You shouldn't pretend to be a folklorist ..."

I smiled, and my mind went to one of the many wise statements that my great-grandmother used when confronted by someone else's opinions. I often mention that when Great-Grandma Essie said, "Bless you", she meant, "Bless you with what you truly deserve."

I almost said, "Bless you." But, instead, because I told myself this man may have had good intentions, I replied, "I've never claimed to be a folklorist. I'm a storyteller, a keeper and adapter of my family's stories. And most of my family's roots lie, or were transplanted, in the Appalachian region.

"If the term, 'Affrilachian' bothers you, you need to look up its history, and its meaning. You'll find the history of the word's creation at the web site of poet and Professor Frank X. Walker[1], as well as at the web site for the Affrilachian Poets[2]. You'll find the etymology and meaning of the word in the New Oxford American Dictionary, second edition. The word is also referenced in The Encyclopedia of Appalachia".

I prepared to turn to others who were waiting to chat, but I blame the trickster portion of my personality for what I said next, "Thank you for trying to preserve the past, although your version is a misinformed one. Bless you." One does not give power to those who attempt to subvert knowledge, simply because it does not fit into their own worldview.

What were the stories I shared that day? Students of American literature and my fellow storytellers know them well. They are the tales some folks call Brer Rabbit stories. That trickster is known simply as Rabbit in my family's versions of these centuries-old stories. Many European-Americans, some in their eighties and nineties, many from my own generation, have told me over the years that they "grew up with these stories." Many teachers, librarians and storytellers have told me they share these stories with their children at home or at school. But some African Americans of my own generation have told me they never heard stories during their formative years. They were never introduced to stories of the trickster-rabbit, or the tortoise, and definitely not stories of the trickster-spider.

Some, born and nurtured in the same cultural heritage as I, have said they were embarrassed to hear the words "brer" and "tar baby" as they grew up. These peers say they only knew these terms as derogatory and denigrating to people of color. They also said they knew nothing of the rich history of these tales, and their direct links to our ancestors from Africa.

In my own family, the Rabbit tales were often dispatched to the back porch, where the older men and their friends told stories the womenfolk felt were too raucous or risqué for neighbors to overhear. My paternal grandmother, Edna Maclin Cooper, once said to my maternal grandfather, Pop-Pops Byard, as well as to her own son, my dad, "You need to stop telling that child those slave stories. We don't need to remember those things." Fortunately for me, her admonition only prompted Dad and Pop-Pops to tell me more stories of the struggles our people faced. Some of their stories were what we would today call historical narratives, and some that also told of our history were told allegorically as the adventures of Rabbit or Spider.

And why do I consider the hearing of those stories such a fortunate thing? The stories gave me roots that I could research in my adult years. I would eventually discover for myself that these stories were carried orally from my ancestors in Africa, were blended with elements of Native American heritage and European American family folktales in Appalachia. Learning these handed-down stories gave me a sense of independence, knowing that size, strength, appearance, and the opinions of others need not deter me from making the choices that made or changed my life. The stories gave me wisdom, dressed up as fables or dressed down as proverb tales. Either way, I came to understand that the stories I heard from old folks were bejeweled with the wisdom of generations. I also came to understand that their ageless values were still potent in the 21st century. The heritage of stories handed down to me became the stories I would tell my own children. They became the grist for my programs. Those back-porch stories continue to be a blessing, passed down through families for centuries.

I heard stories of critters who are now a part of the folktale traditions of these United States: Rabbit, Bear, Turtle, Frog, Dog, Cat, Snake, and Possum. Others appeared in these tales, animals from the memories of those who crossed the oceans in the African Diaspora. These tales included Hyena and his sisters and brothers, or Spider, who was also Ananse.

I heard stories meant to teach me about relationships, empathy and common sense, or the lack of it. Sometimes the protagonists in these stories had names like Jack, or Sistah Sarah Mae, or John. Sometimes they were just Little Girl, or a boy, or an old woman and an old man.

I heard stories that kept me up most of the night, delighting in the images that crept from the shadows of darker folktales into the corners of my room. Daddy told me about spookers and haints and things (pronounced "thangs") that didn't just go bump in the night—they bumped, and thumped, and lost their heads. Oh, how I loved being scared by those stories!

I am grateful to: my father, Edward Maclin Cooper; my mother, Jean Elizabeth Arkward Cooper Matthews; my grandfather, Byard Wilmer Arkward; my great-grandparents, Essie and Jerome Arkward; my great-grandparents' neighbor, Miss Mary; my great-aunt, Katherine Griffin, and many elders whose names I can't remember, for keeping the stories alive and sharing their oral traditions with me. The stories maintain a psycho-spiritual connection to ancestors, traditions of culture and faith, and a history far richer than the schools of my own childhood ever taught. The stories, and their storytellers, helped me to know and become who I am.

I am an Affrilachian storyteller. I pass on a gift of stories to my children, and to you.

1. Frank X. Walker is an associate professor in the Department of English at the University of Kentucky. His visual art is in the private collections of Spike Lee, Opal Palmer Adisa, Morris FX Jeff, and Bill and Camille Cosby. He is also a published poet and playwright, and

one of the founders of the Affrilachian Poets. Walker created the word that now describes people of African descent from the Appalachian region: Affrilachian.

2. Established in 1991, the Affrilachian Poets, based in Louisville, Kentucky, are now more than thirty members strong. Information on the Affrilachian Poets is available at http://www.affrilachianpoets.com/

"AFFRILACHIAN?"
A Personal History

My "Home-Fried Tales," adapted primarily from my family's front-porch and back-porch tales, have afforded me the blessings of telling stories in 29 states and Ireland, of being published in several resources for educators and storytellers, of receiving a few awards, and of having CDs and video and audio recordings on the Internet. I won't dwell on those developments, but if you see me smiling, you'll know the pleasure of serendipity. When my family shared stories, we anticipated nothing of what has become my storytelling career; storytelling was simply the family's tradition for generations.

I will try to give you a taste of the gems that await discovery by those of us who seek family connections to the history of our Appalachian ancestors in this country. Some gems of family lore are lost because folks do not know their families' Appalachian history. Other gems are inadvertently discarded, for whatever reason, when elders are unaware of the value of passing on Appalachian stories in their families.

I speak of my family and myself as "Affrilachian".

My mother's family–Carters, Wilsons, and Arkwards, primarily in Virginia–eventually settled in Pennsylvania and in the hills of Southern Ohio; later, they built a house in a small valley in East Liverpool, Ohio. Ma (born Jean Elizabeth Arkward) says her folks were referred to as "West Virginia ridge-runners", among other derogatory descriptive terms. The heritage of Cherokee and possibly Choctaw was not spoken of, but Great-Pop (Jerome Arkward, my great-grandfather) guided me into the woods for prayer, and I heard a few words that I still remember, which turned out to be Cherokee. Nor did the family speak of the ties to the Carter plantations of Virginia, although my mother and others told me that's where some of the family began, as both indentured servants and people whose bodies were enslaved. I say their bodies were enslaved, because wise folks taught me that nobody can make a slave of your mind and spirit--unless you let them.

In his lifetime, Grandpa Byard Arkward, whom we called Pop-Pops, was a coal miner and a pottery-mill worker at a time when folks of any "color" weren't being hired to work in those factories. At other times he was a cook and maitre d', a stonemason, a carpenter, and a moonshiner who also made beer, root beer, and elderberry wine. In addition, Pop-Pops hand-cranked the best ice cream I ever tasted.

Dad was in the last graduating class of the 477th Bombardment Group of the Tuskegee Airmen, but his battle was on this side of the water, creating an "integrated" military force. Dad always worked two jobs, and we always seemed to be in some kind of financial struggle. Hard times resulted from strikes or layoffs at the steel mills, relatives in need of assistance, a roof in need of patching, or any number of other emergencies. Dad was a brilliant man who played gut-bucket guitar and sang the blues. An athlete and an artist, Dad was also skilled in predicting the weather by watching the clouds and other natural indicators of what was to come. Dad couldn't get a higher-paying job because he was a "colored" man, born in Tennessee, who had some college education but "not enough". His name was Edward Maclin (also "Macklin" and "MacLin") Cooper. He was my favorite storyteller. His recognition as a Tuskegee Airman is listed in the book *Black Knights: The Story of the Tuskegee Airmen*, by Lynn M. Homan and Thomas Reilly (Pelican Publishing Co., 2001). His recognition as an Affrilachian comes only through my storytelling.

A big, family-built cabin stood in East Liverpool, Ohio. Out back was an outhouse that was still in use by my Uncle Cedric Wilson's family when I was growing up. I remember going to church with my great-grandparents, whose Victorian-style house was in the same community, on the "colored" side of town. After church, I went into the woods with my great-grandfather, for silent prayer to the cardinal directions; Great-Pop also taught me to walk silently in the woods ("toe-heel, not like the white folks' heel-toe; you can hear them coming.") We also worked in the garden together, Great-Pop, Great-Grandma Essie (my great-grandfather's second wife), and I. I have forgotten more than I like to admit about gardening, but I remember spirituals we sang as we worked, breakfasts after hoeing, and good food served at the dining room table.

I remember some of the terms used for always-homemade meals: kale & "calf turds" (greens with yams); bastard bread (corn meal or flour mixed with salt, bacon fat, and water, and fried, the equivalent of a flat "fry bread"; the extra meal and bacon fat were the occasional offerings of a plantation owner who couldn't help giving a few more or better supplies to his illegitimate, half-African offspring—thus the term "bastard bread"). And I'll never forget the chant, "lie-roach-ketch-meddlers," sometimes pronounced "lie-roach-ketcha-meddle" by some of Dad's friends, and "nunya"…they both mean "eat it, be glad we got it, and don't ask what it is or where it came from".

There were days of picking dandelion greens, washing and

washing them, and making salads with onions from the garden and vinegar and oil dressing. There were tears over taking dandelion tonic ("to wash out all the bad stuff"), and not being allowed to sip dandelion wine with the big folks. There was sassafras tea early in spring, to thin the "sluggish" blood after winter; there were carefully washed wild violet blooms, dipped in crystal sugar to decorate a special cake. We didn't order a pizza until I was well into high school.

Conversations with fellow Affrilachian storyteller Omope Carter Daboiku[1] jogged my memory about such delicacies as:

Chow-chow - green tomato relish still available in its freshest form from the Pennsylvania Dutch markets;

"Cous-cous", which can be traced to the recipe for "coo coo" from various places in the Caribbean, or "turnmeal" from Jamaica - cornbread in buttermilk, or clabbered-with-vinegar milk;

Chitlins - the small intestines of pigs, cleaned, cooked well, and doused with Louisiana Hot Sauce. A nasty job of cleanin', a fantastic feast for eatin';

Fried green tomatoes, which I still make when I can, and, in Omope's words,

"Our northern gumbo/native combo of okra, corn and tomatoes (cooked together in a skillet) and served with fried catfish. And, one of my aunts actually did eat laundry lump starch during pregnancy... just like at home in Western Africa." That gumbo which both our families enjoyed is what other folks call by a Native-American root-ed name: succotash.

Nothing was wasted. Everything tasted good. We ate it. We were glad we got it. And we didn't ask where it came from.

What were called "healing ways", "the old ways" and "family wisdom" by older folks that I knew were often called hoo-doo, super-stition, witchcraft, and worse, by outsiders. That never seemed to stop folks from asking what to do when medicine and prayer didn't resolve situations that troubled them.

Great-great Grandma Wilhelmina Wells, Pop-Pop's grandmother, was a midwife, a "granny woman" who birthed babies and mixed and traded and passed down remedies and traditions for keeping a body healthy and a home well. Some folks called her a witch, but that didn't keep them from coming to her when the "white folks' medicine", as it was called, didn't work. Brown paper was torn, dampened, and pressed against the skin to suture a wound until it could be bandaged or stitched. Tobacco was spit on a bee sting, and the stinger easily drew out when the nasty stuff was wiped away. Ramps, truly stinking wild leeks, cleared our sinuses and our souls, and cleared a room as well if you ate too much of the stuff...but they tasted so much better than onions. Cod liver oil and castor oil supposedly cured us of...everything!

Add to my short list of remedies a few from the childhood memories of storyteller and actress Ilene Evans[3] of West Virginia: ginger tea, to help young women through, or to, their menstrual cycles; asaphoetida bags (filled with an herb that is also known as Devil's Dung, and its smell befits this name) worn on cords tied around the neck as preventive medicine, beech or birch twigs for cleaning teeth; golden seal for infections, and sage tea "for comfort".

Fellow teller James "Sparky" Rucker[3] of Tennessee told me that his family frowned upon the medicines of "those old root folk" (Sparky's grandfather was a bishop in the Church of God), but he remembered sweet oil being put in his ear to heal an earache—it worked.

Medical research is being done on the value of forest herbs once handpicked by our great-great grandmothers, and the remedies used to soothe and to heal; some of them are the ingredients of medications we use today, including treatments for heart disease, hypertension, and various forms of arthritis. White willow is a source for aspirin's salicylic acid; a mixture of honey and apple cider or products from the gingko tree seems to aid those with arthritic pain.

There are still active practitioners of the old ways; their service is still sought when "modern" medicine doesn't do the job. John Lee of Moncure, in the North Carolina Piedmont, is a healer who combines the heritage of Native American, European, and African folk medicine with spiritual divination. He is of mixed Lumbee, Cherokee, African, Irish, and English descent. Lee was born with a caul (the placental material wrapped around the child or over the child's face), a fact that enhances his reputation as a healer.[2]

I learned how to sweep a house from my great-grandmother and my great-aunt Katherine. I don't mean sweep it clean, although that was important. I mean sweep in good fortune and sweep out trouble, sweep to keep wicked or mean folks or sickness away from the front door and to protect the family. This was also called "blessing" a house. A mixture of salt and herbs was sprinkled around windows and doors before sweeping, to help make it a haven, and a home. Seems like I'm the only one who still remembers some of the old ways, and that has annoyed some family folks who want to distance themselves from the knowledge. I cherish it. I blessed our new home before we set a rug to the floor or moved one piece of furniture into it.

I also learned to listen and watch for the birds and insects, to see if a storm was coming. If the birds stopped singing and seemed to disappear, a big storm was coming. If the flies started "biting" on a hot day, they were getting a meal before they'd have to find shelter from a storm. Dry weather was about to end when the leaves on the trees curled themselves into cups to catch the rain. These were not superstitious beliefs; they were matters of observation and common sense.

The elder healers and other wise elders I knew are gone. The cabin that became the East Liverpool homestead, as well as my great-grandparents' Victorian home, are both gone—victims of highway development. Too many people have died, so research on our family history is becoming a harder and bigger job. And some of our kin have hidden who they are and been lost to the rest of us; with the appearance of our European American ancestors more predominant in their features, some relatives on my father's side of the family left behind their own history, their familial connections, the realities of who they are. They "turned white", or became "passing for white", as folks in our neighborhood said. They tore themselves away from what they considered "poor", "country", and "slave-tale", their own Affrilachian roots.

I know a little about some of them, but I'm not interested in finding or telling their stories right now. I just keep doing my best to seek, remember, research, and tell the old Affrilachian stories, because we need them, for our hearts, and for our children's foundation.

Affrilachia is a 13-state area of 410 counties that is also the Appalachia that, in recent years, is recognizing and claiming its own multicultural diversity. In its hills and valleys, its "criks" and "hollers," rest the origins of many African American family's traditions on this side of the waters. It is a cultural history that is just now being claimed by some as equally important and as interesting as the stories and songs of the Gullah on the eastern coast, and the Black Creole of Louisiana.

Those of us blessed with the oral traditions of African American Appalachia tell our personal Affrilachian stories and all the folktales that we can research and remember. Contemporary scholars are now realizing the many life lessons and moral teachings that harmonize within them. These stories of the trickster-hero Rabbit dance with the ancient tales of Hare and Turtle and Spider, a rich and enriching connection to our families' African heritage that, blessedly for me and for many others, some of our mothers and fathers, some of our grandparents and great-grandparents, some of our teachers and many of our storytellers, did not deny.

1. Omope Daboiku Carter lives in the Cincinnati Area of Ohio. She is a storyteller and actress who has been affiliated with the Ohio Arts Council as an Artist-in-Education since 1990. Omope, too is a child from a multicultural, storytelling family; her family's "cultural shift from Native to Colored" was kept as a family "genealogy" story for four generations, since it occurred in 1920.

As I searched for information about my own family, I discovered that my father, his parents and his siblings, were designated as "white" for two years on the US Census in the 1920s...somebody looked, but didn't ask.

2. http://hubpages.com/hub/African-Slaves-Folk-Remedies

3. Ilene Evans and James "Sparky" Rucker are fellow Affrilachian storytellers. Ilene's work preserves a portion of US history through her dramatizations of the lives of sheroes such as Harriet Tubman.

Ilene also tells folktales and shares workshops, both in her home state of West Virginia and around the world; she has shared her gifts at the Fringe Festival in Edinburg, Scotland, the Women's Universities in Saudi Arabia and Al-Babtain Library in Kuwait. Sparky and his wife, Rhonda, preserve and present music, story, and history from the blues to the songs of the Civil Rights Movement, in a schedule of performances that includes almost every week of the year; among their many venues, Sparky and Rhonda include the Kennedy Center for the Performing Arts, the National Underground Railroad Freedom Center, and the Smithsonian Folklife Festival.

Folktales from the Briar Patch

Have you ever seen a briar patch? It's a thicket of thorny branches, densely interwoven. Few children dare crawl in for fear of emerging with scratches and scrapes over their exposed skin. For hill-country folk, a briar patch may also be called a bramble or blackberry patch, where the thorns are sharp, and the berries are sweet.

Rabbit was born and raised in the briar patch, a metaphor for being born into troubles. But wise and tricky Rabbit knows about troubles; he knows how to avoid thorns and stickers, and how to use the briar patch as shelter and protection from the bullies of the forest. Rabbit knows how to survive in troubles, get out of troubles, or simply leave them alone. The rewards for having such wisdom are as sweet as blackberries.

Folktales gave me lessons for the thorny patches of life. But when I was a child, I didn't know I was learning something. I just knew the stories were as sweet as blackberries.

Critters

I heard fables and pourquoi ("how" or "why") tales from the first moments of storytelling that I can remember. I know these were the purview of my dad and my grandfather more than anyone else. At bedtime, Ma read Aesop's fables to us, and Rudyard Kipling's animal stories; she gave each story depth and wonder through the music and power of her voice. But the fables attributed to Aesop hold very little characterization, very little back story on their protagonist and antagonists. They are wonderful anecdotes, but as a child drawn to the spoken word, I wanted more.

"More" was a possum who could sing, a rabbit who could sit on a front porch or fall in love, a heckling bull frog, a snake who wore a coat of many colors. The polished facets of told stories outshone the polished morality of the fabulous stories in books. I could understand and appreciate the story of "Hare and Tortoise", but I could "see" the story of "Possum and Snake" as if it were a movie in my head.

Now, here I am, putting those spoken-word treasures in a book! Ma is pleased and proud. Daddy is laughing and shaking his head in Heaven.

Possum and Snake

Possum was walking down the road, in a place where he'd lived all his life. Possum started singing to himself: La la, la la la, la da dee dee day-dee do, doo dawdy dawdy...

Well, you can tell Possum wasn't watching where his feet were going. He was so busy singing that he didn't pay any attention where he was stepping until he tripped over something at the bend in the road.

"Oops!!" said Possum, and he looked down to see what had tripped him up. There on the ground was a big rock. And underneath the rock was something Possum had not expected to see.

Underneath the rock was a little...bitty...SNAKE!

Well, Possum's mama and daddy had tried to teach him a lot of things when he was a younger possum. One thing they had always told him was, "Possum, snakes can be trouble. You never know when a snake might bite. If a snake has teeth, a snake will bite.

"That's not good or bad; it's just what a snake can do. But if you fool around with a snake, that can be trouble for you.

"Remember what we're tryin' to teach you, Possum: If you see trouble, and you know it's trouble, just leave trouble alone."

Possum looked down at Snake. He said to himself, "M-hm, trouble."

Possum started to walk away, but Snake said, "Excussse me, Misss-ter Posss-um, would you come over here and help me out jussst a little bit? Would you take this big rock off my back, pleassse?"

Possum's mama and Daddy had told him, if you see trouble and you know it's trouble, just leave trouble alone. But that snake was smiling such a sweet little smile that Possum walked over, reached down, and took the rock off Snake's back. Then he started to walk away again.

But Snake said, "Excussse me, Misss-ter Posss-um, would you come back here and help me out jussst a little more? Sssee, thisss road isss rough, and my ssstomach isss gettin' sssore, and my body isss sssooo c-c-cold. And you have sssuch a nice, warm pocket. Could you pick me up and warm me up in your posssum pocket, pleassse?"

Possum knew what his mama and daddy had told him just as well as you do. But Snake was smiling so sweetly and being so polite that Possum reached down, picked up that snake, and put him in his possum pocket.

Possum stood there and sang to himself: La la, la la la…waiting for Snake to warm up and go away. And whether that snake warmed up or whether he didn't, after a while, he rose up from inside Possum's pocket, and looked Possum in the eye.

"Misss-ter Posss-um," said Snake, "I want to thank you for what you have done for me. I think I'll reward you right now. I think I'll jussst…bite you!"

Then Snake giggled as if he'd told a good joke, "Sss-sss-sss…"

Possum said, "Mr. Snake, I don't see how this is funny at all. I took that rock off your back, I let you warm up in my possum pocket, and you kept smilin' and bein' so polite.

"Why," Possum began to cry, "Why, oh, why are you gonna bite me now?"

Snake smiled, "Didn't your mama and daddy ever teach you anything? A sssnake isss alwaysss a sssnake. Trouble isss alwaysss trouble, even when it's sssmilin' at you, ssso…sssay…goodbye!"

Possum felt so silly and sad. He'd picked up trouble and put it in his possum pocket. What was he going to do?

That's when Possum remembered where he'd been going. He was walking to the home of his good friend, Rabbit. Rabbit always got himself out of trouble by using his head. He never used his fists, because he always used his brain.

Maybe Rabbit could help Possum, too.

Possum sniffled and snuffled, and begged Snake, "I don't really want to say goodbye. But if I have to say it, could I say goodbye to a friend? Please, Mr. Snake, before you bite me, could I go down this road and say goodbye to my best friend, Rabbit? Please? Please? PLEASE?"

Possum begged and cried and cried and begged.

Snake said, "Yesss". Snake figured he'd bite Possum soon, and bite Rabbit, too.

Snake curled up in Possum's pocket, and went to sleep: Sss-sss-sss.

Possum walked down the road toward Rabbit's house. He walked on his tippy-toes, as carefully as he could. He thought that he'd live a bit longer if he let that snake sleep. Possum tippy-toed, tippy-toed, slowly, and quietly.

Rabbit was in his rocking chair, rocking and relaxing on his front porch, when he saw Possum walking toward him in a most unusual way—tippy-toe, tippy-toe, tippy-toe…

Rabbit yelled, "Possum, why are you walkin' like that?"

Possum whispered, "Sh, Rabbit. I'm comin' to see you."

Rabbit yelled, "Walkin' like that? Where are you goin', walkin' like that?"

Possum whispered and whimpered, "Oh, I think I'm going'…to

die!" Possum screeched and squealed and pointed to his pocket.

Rabbit thought Possum was pointing toward his stomach. Rabbit asked, "Oh, my poor friend, do you have collywobbles in your tummy?"

Possum whispered and shook his head, "Nope."

Rabbit asked, "Do you have a fever in your big ol' head?"

Possum whispered and slouched his back, "Nope."

Rabbit asked, "Do you have Arthur-in-your-itis? Do you have Rumors-in-your-tisms? What's wrong, Possum?"

Possum whispered, "Snake's in my pocket."

Rabbit said, "What?"

Possum whimpered, "Snake's in my pocket!"

Rabbit said, "I'm not sure I heard you. What did you say?"

Possum yelled, "There's a snake in my pocket!"

Snake woke up, rose from Possum's pocket, and grinned at Rabbit.

"Oh, Possum!" hollered Rabbit. "There's a snake in your pocket! How did you get a snake in your possum pocket?"

Possum told Rabbit about the rock at the bend in the road, and the snake underneath the rock. Possum told Rabbit that he'd picked up trouble and put it in his own pocket. As he told his story, Possum winked at Rabbit, and tried to give some kind of signal for help.

Rabbit said, "No, I can't believe this. I can't see how this could happen."

"But if you take me to where all this happened (and Rabbit winked at Possum), and you show me how it happened (and Rabbit winked again), maybe I'll understand a little better.

"Would that be okay with you, Snake?" asked Rabbit.

Snake didn't care if they went back up the road. Snake figured he'd bite Possum soon, and bite Rabbit, too.

Snake curled up in Possum's pocket again, and went to sleep: Sss-sss-sss.

Possum and Rabbit made their way back up the road. At the bend in the road sat that big rock.

Rabbit shouted, "Snake, wake up! Now, Possum, show me, where were you standing when you put Snake in your pocket?"

Possum said, "Well, I was standing right here." He pointed to a place near the big rock, and he stood there.

Rabbit said, "Now, Snake, show me where you were."

Snake slithered from Possum's pocket, slid to the ground, settled himself near the big rock, and said, "I wasss sssiting right here."

Rabbit picked up the rock and put it on Snake's back. Rabbit said, "There you are again, Snake! And there you will stay. I don't know how you got there, but I do know my friend doesn't know anything about snakes.

"Possum should've left you alone, Snake. After all, you can be trouble."

Then Rabbit took his friend Possum's hand and walked back toward his home. Rabbit kept telling Possum the same thing his own mama and daddy had tried to teach him:

If you see trouble, and you know it's trouble, just leave trouble alone.

Story Notes

Variants of this story are found among the tales of many cultures. After hearing me tell at a local library, a story-listener whose family came from Egypt told me of a similar tale of a crocodile and a merchant. The merchant, hearing the piteous crocodile cry of his looming death in a dry riverbed, carries the devious creature to a river; at the river, the crocodile snaps his jaws, and the merchant's robe is caught in the crocodile's mouth. A little boy, claiming that he cannot understand how such a thing could happen, convinces the crocodile that he should be carried back to the beginning of the adventure—the outcome is a forlorn crocodile in a dry riverbed, and a grateful merchant escorting a little boy to his home.

For me, the story begins with Pop-Pops, Grandpa Byard Arkward, and an afternoon of making strawberry ice cream on the back porch of his home in Sharon, Pennsylvania. The story was good, but the ice cream was even better, and I got the first lick, straight from the dasher in the ice-cream churn.

Why Possum's Tail is Bare

In the times when the world was still kind of new, folks started acting as if their mamas and papas had never taught them to behave. They were mean and nasty, wild and terrible. They didn't appreciate their blessings. The Good Lord decided the world needed some tidying up. So He told the angels to empty the rain barrels He kept beside the Pearly Gates, but not before He told the only good man on Earth how to survive.

Next thing you know, there was a big flood, waters pouring out of the sky and covering the land. Pretty soon, everything was under water, except for a big boat made by that good man named Noah and his family. They built that boat quick and fine, from a blueprint straight from Heaven. And before they holed up inside that boat, ready for the flood, Noah did what the Good Lord had told him to do. Noah called all the critters to come inside and settle in that boat, and the critters came, big and small, two by two, just before the big rain fell.

It rained and it rained, and the rivers and the seas rose up, washed the world all new and clean again. But that took a while, forty days and forty nights. And while that boat was rocking on the waters, things got kind of boring for the folks stuck inside it.

The people and the critters started getting grumpy and grouchy and pouty and mean, like the folks that had gotten cleaned away in the flood. Noah knew he had to do something about it.

Noah called everybody together and said, "Children, we got to do something to entertain ourselves until this big rain is over. I've decided that, every day, when the work of keeping this boat together is done, we'll take turns entertaining one another. Doesn't matter whether you have two legs, four legs, or no legs at all. If you're in this boat, you're in this business.

"You can dance, or sing, or tell stories, whatever you can do. That's the way we'll pass the time until we can get out of this water and off this boat."

Everybody thought it was a good idea, and everybody agreed to take a turn entertaining the passengers and crew on Noah's boat. Everybody started making plans for what he or she might do to bring some joy to others.

Everybody, except for Mr. Possum. Mr. Possum didn't want to do anything but sleep. He had a long tail covered with a fine tangle of stringy hairs in those days. When Possum was supposed to help with work, he found himself a place to hide, covered himself with that blanket of a tail, and went to sleep. And that's what Possum intended to do whenever his turn to entertain came around.

And it did. But nobody could find Mr. Possum. He'd squeezed himself behind some of the spare wood, set there for patching any holes in that big boat. There he lay, looking like nothing more than a pile of gray cobwebs and string. And there he stayed.

Well, one of Noah's sons, the one named Ham, volunteered to take Possum's place. That day, Ham gathered a bit of that spare wood. He cut himself a long piece, and a couple round pieces, and some pegs and such, and put them all together. Then Ham took some of the string his mama, Mrs. Noah, had used to tie up herbs and tie down supplies. Ham stretched that string around the pegs and a little piece of wood on one of those round pieces. Next thing you knew, that child had made himself the very first banjo.

Ham started practicing, plinkety-plinkety, plucking on those strings, until he could make some noise. He worked at it all afternoon, until that noise turned into music. The music was so fine, folks forgot about what they were doing. Soon everybody was dancing to the tunes from Ham's banjo.

Ham played hard, plinkety-plunk, plunkety-plink, then—Snap! One of those strings broke. Ham looked around for another string. He saw a pile of cobwebs and long strings behind some stacks of wood. Ham yanked out one of those strings, and stretched it on the banjo. That string played better than any of the others. And the music started up again.

But—SNAP! There went another string. Ham yanked a new one out of that pile of cobwebs and string. The music went on, with folks stomping and laughing, clapping hands and paws, tapping tails and toes. Every time Ham broke a string, he knew where to find another one. And, even with all that jumping and jiving going on, Possum never woke up.

Some say that party went on all day and night and right into the next day and night, until folks were too tired to dance anymore. And some folks say the party went on until that big boat bumped against something, and Noah opened the door to see dry land and a rainbow.

However long the party went on, Mr. Possum didn't wake up until it was over. See, he felt cold, thought his tail had flipped off his back and slumped toward the floor. When he couldn't reach it in his sleep, Mr. Possum woke himself up, and saw what was left of his tail.

That thing was almost gone, not a hair hanging off of it, just a long, pink ratty thing, the tail that possums wear to this very day.

When Mr. Possum saw that, he fainted.

Possums have been fainting ever since. When they see somebody coming toward them, they figure it's somebody ready to snatch off what's left of that tail. But that fine stringy tail is gone.

This tale is gone, too.

Story Notes

For some folks in my family, spirituality was a close walk with the Good Lord. He wasn't far away from most of my elder relatives. He was in the garden with Great-Grandma every spring, summer, and fall; planting time, weeding time, harvest time, she talked to him all the time: "Good Lord! My knees hurt! Now, God, I know you got your hand on my shoulder every day, but maybe you should put it on my knees for a while this morning. They could use a little help."

Some folks called on the Good Lord as if He were a relative, or a friend as close as family. Prayer was a conversation, a routine part of the day, and the people of the Good Book were referred to as if they were friends and family, too.

Daddy told pourquoi (French for "how" or "why") tales about the Good Lord and the folks of the Bible, but never within earshot of the preachers or Sunday School teachers in the family, including my mother. I heard most of them when he and I were going places in the car, or coming home from the many chores he did for people in the community. I found out Pig's nose got flattened because he wouldn't keep it out of other folks' business, and Spider can't make colorful thread because he tried to steal the fine threads of Snake's coat.

Daddy said these were stories nobody believed, "but they told them anyway."

Frog and Rabbit

Once upon a time, about time-and-a-half ago, Frog and Rabbit were hopping buddies, but not the best of friends.

Every day, from sunrise to sunset, Frog and Rabbit hopped and worked together in the garden between their houses. They turned the soil, pulled the weeds, and planted the seeds together; they grew fine vegetables of every color and kind.

All that working together should've made them good friends. But every day, first thing in the morning, Rabbit made Frog angry.

You see, the two had decided they'd take turns making breakfast for one another. One morning, Frog made breakfast at his house; the next morning, Rabbit made breakfast at his house.

No matter who made breakfast, Rabbit ate everything—slurp, gobble, GULP!

Frog made breakfast at his house. Slurp, gobble, GULP! Rabbit ate everything.

Rabbit made breakfast at his house. Slurp, gobble, GULP! Rabbit ate everything.

Frog made breakfast at his house, but he fussed, and yelled and screamed, and hopped up and down as if his toes were on fire. Didn't matter. Slurp, gobble, and GULP! Rabbit ate everything.

Then one evening, hungry and angry, Frog came up with a plan to teach greedy Rabbit a lesson. Long after the work was done, Frog hopped over to Rabbit's house, and banged on the door, BLIM! BLAM! BLIM!

When Rabbit saw Frog at his door, he figured Frog had come over for a fight about breakfast. But Frog said, "Rabbit, I have a surprise for you. No matter whose turn it is to make breakfast tomorrow morning, I've decided that I'll make breakfast at my house."

Rabbit pulled his whiskers. "You'll make breakfast, Frog? Well, fine," Rabbit said. "That's fine!"

"Yep," Frog said, "I'm gonna make your favorite meal, a big pot of vegetable stew, with the freshest vegetables from our garden."

Rabbit scratched his ears. "My favorite? Vegetable stew? Well, fine," Rabbit said. "That's really fine!"

"Yep," Frog said, "but, there's some early-morning work to be done in the garden, some young plants I need to tend. I have to cover them tonight, so they don't freeze in the late-night chill, and uncover them early tomorrow, for the day-bright sun. I might be busy in the garden when you come to breakfast, but I'll leave my door unlocked, just for you.

"If I'm not at the table, you just help yourself to breakfast. Rabbit, you eat all you want."

Rabbit grinned as he said, "Eat all I want. And you won't be there? Well, fine! That's just fine!"

"Yep," Frog said, and he grinned, too, all the way back to his own house.

When Frog got home, he started a fire in his cook stove, not too much tinder, not too much wood, just enough heat to make a pot simmer. Then Frog reached into his cupboard, and pulled out the biggest cooking pot he had.

Frog set that pot on the cook stove, and poured a little water into it. Then Frog added fresh vegetables from the garden: green beans, collard greens, kale and cabbage, spinach and corn, sweet yams, red onions and white onions, peas and carrots, fine vegetables of every color and kind.

The vegetables simmered as Frog stirred the pot. Frog watched it bubble all night long. The vegetables slowly cooked, into a good-smelling, strange-looking vegetable mush.

Frog took the pot off the cook stove, and set it on the table. Frog set out two bowls, and two spoons. When the vegetable mush had cooled a bit, Frog jumped up on the table, hopped onto the rim of that big cooking pot, held his breath, and dropped into the pot— SPLOOCH!

Frog waited. Finally, he heard Rabbit banging on his door, BLIM! BLAM! BLIM!

When Frog didn't come to the door, Rabbit let himself in for breakfast. There on the table were two bowls, and two spoons, and a pot of something that looked kind of strange, but smelled like delicious vegetable stew.

"This stew looks mooshy-ooshy, but I didn't have to cook it. And Frog's not here; I can eat all I want. Well, fine!" Rabbit smiled, "That's just fine!"

Rabbit didn't use his spoon or table manners. He just sat down and picked up a bowl, scooped up some mush, and swallowed, slurp, gobble, GULP! That mushy stuff was so delicious, Rabbit scooped out some more. Slurp, gobble, GULP!

"More!" Rabbit giggled, and slurp, gobble, GULP! Rabbit emptied the pot, and licked it clean.

Well, you know how it is when your belly gets full. Rabbit felt like taking a nap. He wanted to go home and sleep. But as Rabbit rose from his chair, his belly r-r-rumbled and gr-gr-grumbled. It rolled to one side of his body, then the other.

Rabbit thought he had to burp. He opened his mouth, and up from his throat came, "Burrp—greedy—greedy—greedy!"

"Oops," said Rabbit to himself, "excuse me." He took a few steps toward the door. His belly r-r-rumbled and gr-gr-grumbled. It rolled to one side, then the other. "Ow!" said Rabbit, and right behind that "Ow", up from Rabbit's throat came, "Barrp—greedy—greedy—greedy!"

"Oh, my belly!" Rabbit moaned. He tried to run down the road to his own house. But every time he took a step, his stomach r-r-rumbled and gr-gr-grumbled. It rolled to one side, then the other, and noises came from Rabbit's throat, whether he meant to say anything or not: Burrp—greedy—greedy—greedy! Barrp—greedy—greedy—greedy! BURRP—greedy—greedy—GREEDY!

Rabbit fell to the ground. He rolled all around. He held his stomach. He opened his mouth, and moaned, "Owww, ooohh, I shouldn't have been so greedy!"

And right then, out of Rabbit's open mouth hopped Frog.

"Yep," Frog said, "That's right, Rabbit. You should not have been so greedy, greedy, greedy!" Frog turned his back, and hopped home.

Rabbit jumped up and ran, lickety-split, all the way to his house. And, ever since then, frogs and rabbits have not been friends, not even hopping buddies.

You see, to this very day, frogs sit in the forest or around the ponds and streams in the evening, and talk about that selfish rabbit, and the way he ate. If you sit quietly in the woods, you can hear them saying, "Greedy—greedy—greedy."

The rabbits know the story, because the frogs keep telling it. Embarrassed rabbits don't slurp and gobble and gulp their food anymore. When rabbits eat, they take tiny little nibbles of everything.

Rabbits remember the time that other rabbit had a frog in his throat.

Story Notes

"About time and a half ago…" was my grandfather's way of saying "Once upon a time…" "Pop-Pops" Byard Arkward was the second-best storyteller I ever heard. I begin my version of this story with his words.

My favorite storyteller was my father, whom friends and family called "Jake. I don't remember who first told me this tale of the less-than-friendly neighbors, Frog and Rabbit, so I share this version, my own adaptation, to honor both Pop-pops and Daddy.

Greed has its own price to pay. Frog teaches that lesson to Rabbit in a funny but rather disgusting way. The same lesson is taught in a very similar tale from Ghana, related in Jack Berry's collection, *West African Folk Tales* (Northwestern University, 1991). In this story, Frog's wife serves a meaty stew to greedy Spider (undoubtedly a relative of the beloved Akan culture-hero and trickster, Anansi), who swallows Frog, hidden in the meat his wife has served; after forty days of stomach troubles and strange sounds—"Greedeep! Greedeep!" or "Woya" in the Adengme language, as Berry explains in his "Notes"—Frog reappears through Spider's mouth, and chastises Spider.

Good stories travel far, and live as long as they are told. May this adaptation of my elders' story travel, as a friend, with those who read and enjoy it.

Fox and Old Man Turtle

Fox was a sly and hungry fellow, liked to sneak up on smaller critters and snatch 'em away for a meal.

Sometimes Fox had a taste for rabbit stew, or roast squirrel, and sometimes he got a taste for frog legs, or a bowl of turtle soup. That's when he'd saunter down to the pond. He'd bully the bullfrogs and tease the tiny frogs sitting in and around the water; he'd snap at them and paw at them, and sometimes he'd catch a few. Then he tormented Old Man Turtle, tried to catch him by a leg or by his head or tail, and yank him out of his shell so he could turn that poor turtle into soup.

Old Man Turtle had been around for a long time. He'd learned a few tricky ways from the best of tricksters, Rabbit, and Old Man Turtle had some tricks of his own, too. When Fox snapped at him and scratched at him with those paws and claws, Old Man Turtle pulled his arms and legs, his head, and his tail deep inside his shell—bloop! Fox could snap and paw all he wanted then, but he couldn't get to Old Man Turtle inside that shell. Fox would give up his hungry hunt, and go into the woods to try and find the fixings for rabbit stew or roast squirrel.

One morning, Old Man Turtle was making his way back from a nearby field. He'd gone there to snack on the bugs that nibbled at the blades of sweet grass and the tasty clover. But there'd been some trouble in that field, big trouble that Old Man Turtle hadn't expected. And now, Old Man Turtle was heading to the pond, walking slower than ever. Sometimes he stopped altogether, shook his little head and said, "Ow."

Old Man Turtle took a few steps, stopped, shook his head, and said, "Ow," again. Then he thought about the way he was walking, and the one he might meet on the way back home.

"Oh, I hope this is the day that Fox leaves me alone," moaned Old Man Turtle. "I'm too tired and too sore to have to deal with him today. I just want to get back to my home in the pond."

And who do you think came down the road right then? That's right. Fox.

Fox trotted along, sniffing up a bite to eat. When he saw Old Man Turtle, he stopped trotting and started running. "Aaah," Fox grinned as he ran. "Time for turtle soup!"

Well, Old Man Turtle pulled himself into his shell—bloop! But something was wrong with his tail. It was all crispy and crooked, and it wouldn't slide all the way into the shell like it should. Old Man Turtle's tail just bent kind of funny, and crackled.

"OW!" shouted Old Man Turtle. Then he started to cry, but he kept his head inside his shell.

Fox heard that turtle cry, and he stopped. Seemed like old Man Turtle had a problem.

Fox asked, "Old Man Turtle, what's wrong with you? Why you makin' such a terrible noise?"

Turtle lamented, "This has been a bad day, Fox. And I wish you'd just leave me alone.

"I went to the field to have myself a snack. Then I heard the farmer talkin' 'bout clearin' the field to do some plantin'. I didn't know that meant he was gonna set the field afire! Next thing I knew, my toes were heatin' up, and my shell was getting' singed, and my tail, oh, I think it's burnt like bacon!"

Fox looked at that turtle's tail. Sure enough, it was still sizzling, and it wouldn't curl up and slide inside Old Man Turtle's shell.

"Oh, you poor thing," said Fox. "Don't worry. I'll take care of you. Why, I'll…just…

"Snatch you up by that crispy tail and shake you right outta that shell!"

Fox grabbed Old Man Turtle's burnt up tail and started shaking him left and right.

"OW!" cried Old Man Turtle. But he knew yelling and crying wouldn't get him out of this predicament. He'd have to be as tricky as a turtle could be, maybe even as tricky as Rabbit.

"Fox, you can shake me 'til I fall outta this shell. You can take me home and make me into soup. But, please, don't throw me into the pond!"

"Uh, what?" asked Fox. He stopped shaking the turtle, but he kept hold of that tail. "Why, I thought you liked the water!" he said.

"Well, generally speakin', I do", said Old Man Turtle. "But I'm so hot from that fire that I'll probably boil in the water. I don't want to boil to death. Please, whatever you do, don't throw me into the pond!"

Just to be mean, Fox said, "Ha! I think that's what I'm gonna do, Turtle. I'm gonna throw you into the pond, and let you boil. Then I'm gonna have boiled turtle for dinner!"

"No! Please! Don't do it!" begged Old Man Turtle. But he was looking forward to the cool water, and the shelter of the pond that was his home.

Fox trotted down to the pond, and threw Old Man Turtle into the water—splash!

Old Man Turtle sank right down to the bottom, where he settled into the cool, soothing mud. And there he stayed, letting his toes be tickled by the waters, his singed shell cool off, and his crispy-bacon tail heal.

Fox waited for that turtle to start bubbling and boiling. But nothing happened. That is, nothing happened except that Fox figured out he'd been tricked.

Fox jumped up and down, fussing and fuming and shouting, "You old hard-backed hustler! You tricked me! I don't believe you did that!"

Fox jumped up and down, and fell into the pond—SPLASH! And Old Man Turtle bit that young Fox's tail—SNAP!

"YOW!"

Now it was Fox's turn to cry. He splashed and spluttered, and leaped out of the pond.

The bullfrogs and the little frogs started laughing at Fox. The biggest bullfrog called out, "Turtle gotcha. Turtle gotcha! I don't believe it! I don't believe it!"

Fox was so embarrassed, he didn't even try to catch any of the frogs. He didn't hunt for rabbits or squirrels, either. Fox just went home.

Frogs, big and small, told any critter who would listen about the way Old Man Turtle had tricked Fox. Then the little frogs giggled, "duh-dee, duh-dee, duh-dee", and the bull frogs puffed themselves up and praised Old Man Turtle.

To this day, if you go to the pond, you can hear the frogs still talking about tricky Old Man Turtle and foolish Fox, and still laughing. The little frogs giggle, "duh-dee, duh-dee, duh-dee." And the bullfrogs tell the story and brag, "Turtle did it. Believe it. Turtle did it. Believe it!"

Story Notes

Great-Grandpa Jerome Arkward, "Great-Pops," told this story after I'd spent some time in "the stone pond," a pool he'd built next to the old Victorian house where I spent many lovely days each summer. The pool was a round stone wall filled with water, in which swam what I thought were the biggest goldfish in the world. I didn't know they were koi, or that the stone pond was actually a pool. Orange and golden and speckled, those fish drifted like dreams in the water that rippled over a deep blue concrete floor.

Late one summer, Great-Pop told me that we were going to clean out the pool. "We have to catch the fish first," he said.

He went toward the shed, but he returned quickly when I started yelling for help.

I'd taken his words seriously, climbed into the pool, and managed to catch one of those big goldfish. I'd wrapped my arms tightly around the thing, and lifted it out of the water. I don't know how I managed that, but I do know I was afraid to let go. That fish was a squirmy thing, and its tail was slapping me in the face.

"Help! I cried. I probably sounded like Fox. But Great-Pop was no help at all. He was laughing so hard he couldn't make a sound. When he could, he gave me the simplest of instructions: "Lynnie, let go!"

I did. Problem solved. Then he helped me out of the pool, and we got his wading boots, the net, and the buckets from the shed.

Somehow, my foolishness reminded Great-Pops of this story. I remember sitting on the edge of the stone pond as he stood in the water, scooped giant goldfish into buckets of water, and told me about Fox falling into Old Man Turtle's pond.

Turtle Wants to Fly

Back in the days when turtles had smooth shells, young Turtle wandered through the forest. He sniffled and he snuffled. He whined and he pouted. He fussed and he cried.

Turtle made so much noise, he woke up little sparrows who were trying to take a nap. They flew down from their nests in the maple trees. They fluttered around Turtle. They asked, "Turtle, what is your problem?"

Turtle said, "Turtle wants to fly!"

The sparrows tried not to laugh, but that was the silliest thing they'd ever heard.

The sparrows chirped, "Turtle, you're not supposed to fly. To fly, you need feathers and wings, and you don't have those things.

"But you have gifts no bird has. You carry your home on your back. When it rains, you just slide inside. You're never lost or far from home. Be happy being Turtle."

But Turtle shook his head in disagreement. He cried out, "Turtle wants to fly!"

He sniffled and he snuffled. He whined and he pouted. He fussed and he cried.

The sparrows gave up on making Turtle feel better. They went back to their nests, pulled their heads close to their chests, and tried to get some sleep.

Turtle walked back toward his family's pond. When he got there, his sisters and brothers were asleep in the sunlight that warmed their resting place, the rocks at the edge of the water.

Turtle sniffled and he snuffled. He whined and he pouted. He fussed and he cried. Soon, all the little turtles were awake.

"Brother, what is wrong with you?" they all asked.

Turtle said, "Turtle wants to fly!"

The other turtles tried not to laugh, but that was the silliest thing they'd ever heard.

They said, "Oh, Brother, we're not supposed to fly! To fly, we need feathers and wings, and you know we just don't have those things.

"But we can do things that nobody else can do. We carry our homes on our backs. When it rains, we just slide inside. We're never lost or far from home. Be happy being one of us."

But Turtle shook his head, and said, "Turtle wants to fly!"

He sniffled and he snuffled. He whined and he pouted. He fussed and he cried. He made so much noise that his sisters and brothers drew themselves into their shells, and tried not to listen.

So Turtle walked back into the forest. And you know what he did. Yes, he sniffled and he snuffled. He whined and he pouted. He fussed and he cried.

Turtle made so much noise, nobody in the forest could take a nap.

Two big blackbirds flew down. One settled on the left side of Turtle. The other sat down on his right side. Turtle figured he was about to become dinner.

But the blackbirds flapped their wings and called, "All this noise! Why do you make all this noise?"

You know what Turtle said? Yep… "Turtle wants to fly!"

"If we help you fly, if we take you into the sky," said one of the birds, "do you promise that, when we bring you back down, you'll keep your big mouth shut?"

Turtle grinned, and nodded, shouted, "Turtle wants to fly!"

The other blackbird said, "Here's what we'll do. We'll bring you a stick. You hold it in your mouth. We'll carry the stick into the sky. And as we rise, you will fly."

Turtle watched the two blackbirds fly to a nearby tree. They broke off a thin branch, and tore off the leaves and twigs. Then they brought that branch to Turtle.

Turtle opened his mouth and clamped it shut on that stick— clomp!

The blackbirds grasped the stick in their talons. They flapped their great wings, and slowly rose higher and higher.

Turtle felt the wind beneath his shell. He kept his mouth tightly shut, but he tilted his head just enough to see the earth far below his little feet.

Turtle was flying!

The blackbirds carried Turtle over the trees where the little sparrows were sleeping. Turtle tried to get their attention. He wanted them to see that he could fly just like the birds.

With his mouth clamped shut on that stick, Turtle called out:

"Hmm! Hmmm mm mm! M hmm hmm!"

The sparrows didn't hear a thing. They were fast asleep.

The blackbirds carried Turtle to his family's pond. The turtles were resting, with their heads drawn into their shells. But Turtle wanted his brothers and sisters to see that he could do something no other turtle could do.

Still holding onto that stick, Turtle called out:

"Hmm! Hmmm mm mm! M hmm hmm!"

But nobody paid any attention to him. He tried again:

"HMM! HMMM MM MM! M HMM HMM!"

Not one turtle looked into the air. Turtle got upset. He got angry. He wanted folks to see what he could do, and nobody would even look at him. Turtle got so frustrated, he let go of that stick, and shouted:

"I SAID, HEY! LOOK AT ME. I CAN…uh…uh, oh…

"I can't fly," said Turtle as he flapped his arms as hard as he could. "But…I…can…

"FALL!"

Turtle fell to the ground—whack! He landed on his back—crack! And Turtle broke his shell into the cracked one that turtles wear to this very day.

Ever since then, turtles have worn cracked shells. But they don't mind. Those shells remind them that they should be happy being who they are. After all, turtles carry their homes on their backs. When it rains, they just slide inside. They're never lost, or far from home.

Turtles also know something that storytellers need to remember: sometimes, when you have something to say, it's okay to shout loudly and proudly. But sometimes it's better to keep your big mouth shut.

Story Notes

There are two obvious morals in this story. The first, of course, is an encouragement to be contented being who you are. The second, and probably the more important lesson for a little chatterbox child (and I was one when there were no strangers around), was to know when to speak, and when to shut up.

This is the only folktale that I can attribute first to my great-grandfather, "Great-Pop" Jerome Arkward, then to my dad, his grand-son-in-law. In those days of political incorrectness, Great-Pop would say, "This came from the Indians in the family." Dad said, "This is a story my father told me when I was a child." I have no proofs for where and when either of them heard the story, but my research has shown me that versions of both "Fox and Old Man Turtle" and "Turtle Wants to Fly" are part of the rich story heritage of the Chero-kee people. Dad said part of the family was "Cherokee-Choctaw", but he never talked much about any part of his family.

Great-Pop and Dad would walk into the woods, with me close at hand as they talked about what their folks "used to do". In those woods in East Liverpool, Ohio, Great-Pop taught me a little about tracking, and a lot about the importance of stillness, silent prayer, ob-servation, and respect for the woods. Oh, how I wish I had learned more.

Why Dog Chases Cat

Once upon a time, about time-and-a-half ago, Dog and Cat lived together like brothers. And you know that sometimes brothers are nothing alike. Dog liked to eat and run. Cat liked to eat, clean himself, and sleep. Dog liked to bark and play. Cat liked to stretch, and sleep. Sometimes Dog chased after Cat, until Cat found a place to hide, and sleep. Sometimes Cat chased mice, or birds, or a piece of string hanging from the sofa cover. Most of the time, Cat liked to sleep.

Dog thought Cat was lazy. Cat thought Dog was silly. Brotherhood between the two of them was bound to end.

One day, Dog came home with a big chunk of meaty ribs that the farmer had given him. He said, "Cat, I brought home dinner. Since I got it for us, you should cook it for us."

Cat yawned, and stretched. Then Cat said, "Brother Dog, I'm just too sick to cook for us. My back aches, my ears itch, and my teeth feel funny. Maybe you can cook the meat for us this time, and I'll do it next time." Cat climbed onto the sofa, and lay there.

Dog felt sorry for Cat. And Cat had called him "brother." So Dog got the barbecue grill going and he cooked up those ribs.

Well, Cat might've been sick, but not too sick to eat. When the ribs were ready, Cat jumped off the sofa and greedily snatched away a piece of that meat. Cat ran off and ate alone. He didn't come back to the house until the dishes were done and put away.

Dog said, "Brother Cat, I did the food-findin', and the cookin', and the cleanin' up after it. Tomorrow, you bring home some kind of supper for us, and you cook it, and you clean the kitchen."

Cat licked his paws, cleaned his ears, curled up on the sofa, and went to sleep.

The next morning, Dog couldn't find Cat anywhere. He barked and barked, "Cat! Your turn to rustle up some supper for us today! Cat?"

Cat stayed away all day, so Dog went hunting. Dog brought home a squirrel for supper.

When he walked in the door, there was Cat, asleep on the sofa again.

Dog dropped that squirrel and shouted, "Cat! I did the hunting. You get up and get our supper ready!"

Cat rolled off the sofa, and flopped on his back on the floor. "Brother Dog," Cat said, "Didn't you notice that I was gone all day? Why, I had to find some wild grass and mint to make my poor stomach feel better. My knee-bones are bent, and my eyes are all squinty. I can't even see well enough to know what you brought home for supper. Please, Brother Dog, you cook supper this time, and I'll do it next time." Cat climbed back up on the sofa, and lay there.

Well, Dog had a big heart. Cat had called him "brother" again, and Cat's knees did look bent.

Dog skinned and cleaned and boiled up that squirrel in a simenjous* pot, with onions and potatoes. Oh, it smelled wonderful!

Dog didn't even have to call Cat to the table. Snatch! Cat grabbed what he wanted and took off again. Cat didn't come back until the pot was washed and clean, and the kitchen was clean, too.

Dog growled, "Cat, you don't treat me like a brother. Tomorrow, no matter how you feel, you are going to bring home the meal. You are going to cook it, and you are going to clean the kitchen!"

Cat twitched his tail a little, pawed at the sofa cushions until they were nice and soft, and went to sleep.

The next day, Dog got up earlier than the sun. He tiptoed from his little bed and down to the sofa, just in time to see Cat trying to sneak out the door.

Dog leaped in front of that door, and said, "If you go anywhere, Cat, you better come back with supper!"

"That's just what I was about to do," Cat purred. "Even though I feel terrible, I intend to bring home something, Brother Dog."

Dog stepped aside, and let Cat go through the door. But he thought about the way things had been going between him and Cat.

Cautiously, Dog asked, "Cat, what you think you'll bring home for supper?"

Cat grinned, and said, "My appetite!" Then Cat took off running.

Well, Dog ran right after Cat, chased him around the yard, and around the house, and around the farm, and right into the forest. And Dog has been chasing Cat ever since.

Story Notes

An African American folktale speaks of Cat tricking Dog into dropping a ham, by convincing Dog to sing about the meaty treasure they are about to share. When Dog sings, "Our ham, our ham," he drops the ham. Cat steals it, and runs up a tree with it, where Cat sings out, "My ham, my ham." This is given as the reason why Dogs chase Cats.

My Pop-Pops' version made more sense to me, a sister with two younger siblings, each with a distinct personality that didn't always synchronize with mine. We didn't always get along, but we always remembered we were family for one another. And I didn't chase my sister and brother, except in games of tag. I climbed our cherry tree, and sat in its branches, where I ate cherries, ripe and tart in the last days of summer, and read a book.

*simenjous – Pop-pops' word for "stupendous" and "tremendous". He knew both words, but his made-up adjective made me laugh.

Look Every
Which-A-Way

Once upon a time, about time-and-a-half ago, there was this rabbit, thought he was tricky. Folks called him "brother", but sometimes he was in it all for himself.

One evening the rain poured down on him so hard he could hardly see. Ran into the first open door he could find. Shook himself off. Saw Wolf sitting on the outside, with him on the inside of Wolf's house.

Rabbit said, "Oh, Lord, what have I done? Lord, why did you let me run this way?"

Wolf said, "You prayin'? Well, I'll pray, too: Thank God the rain done sent some meat in my door. Gonna grab that rabbit, gonna eat him soon. Gonna feed my face by the light of the moon. Thank God, the rain done sent some meat in my door. Hah!"

Rabbit looked for a back door to get out of Wolf's house. Wolf's house didn't have one. Rabbit looked for windows to jump out. Wolf's house didn't have windows, either. Rabbit looked for a fireplace with a chimney hole. Wolf's house didn't even have a fireplace with a chimney hole.

"Rabbit asked, "Wolf, how you live like this? This ain't nothing but a box with a roof on it!"

Wolf said, "Might not be much, but it's enough t'keep you from getting' away. Thank God, the rain done sent some meat in my door! Hah!"

Wolf heard lots of scratching and scratching, but he didn't pay much attention to it. Rabbit wouldn't find a way to get out of his house.

After a long while, the rain stopped. Wolf went on in his house to get that Rabbit.

Rabbit was gone. No back door, no windows, no chimney, but Rabbit had gotten away from that ol' wolf again.

Wolf yelled out into the evening air, "Rabbit, where you at?"

He couldn't see Rabbit, but he heard Rabbit say, "Outside and down the road, and I'm praying again! Thank God, a big rat put a hole in your floor! Gonna go on home, gonna get there soon, 'cause I found a way to get outta that room. Thank God a big rat put a hole in your floor! HAH!"

See, Rabbit got himself into that trouble. He got himself out, too. Lots of ways to get yourself out of a mess. You just got to remember to look every which-a-way until you find the way out.

Story Notes

This was one of Pop-pops' "knee-to-knee" stories, the ones he usually shared with an audience of one, me. Some folks called them "slave tales"—"Don't tell that child those 'slave tales'; we left that shame behind a long time ago"–or "low tales", stories for and from folks with no education and little to no money. This was in the 1950s, when some of the past was a whisper, and the present could be dangerous. Some of the older folks, closer to the times and truths of enslavement and the scenes of lynchings, as well as friends and neighbors who had more recently moved from the South, seemed to think that the future lay in leaving old ways, and old stories, in the past.

Religion was a tie that lovingly bound folks together. Church was home, and the place of foundation for hope. Church was also a meeting hall for discussions of equal rights, and plans for change. But I think I built a foundation for my life just as much from what Pop-pops and Daddy shared in storytelling as I did from the parables and prophetic sermons in church.

One of these two men (oh, Lord, my brain! I just can't remember which one of them said it!) told me, "God gives you strength, possibility, opportunity, and at least a grain of common sense; it's up to you to choose which way you run with that." I'm sure Daddy said, because he said it so often in his stories of the trickster-hero, "Rabbit always used his head, never his fists. He always used his brain to get himself out of trouble."

Amen.

Hyena and the Big Cheese

Long ago, hyenas did not look the way they do today. They had long, straight, strong legs, and straight backs; their fur was golden, with nary a spot anywhere on it. And Big Brother Hyena was the biggest and best-looking hyena of them all.

In those days, there was a drought. Rain didn't fall. There wasn't a cloud in the sky. The sun shone so brightly that it dried up all the earth. The hyenas needed food and water, and so did all the other animals.

Big Brother Hyena called his sisters and brothers and cousins and others together: "Hey, come here!"

All the little hyenas came to see what Big Brother Hyena had to say.

"Follow me," commanded Big Brother Hyena. "I will lead you to food and water."

"Do you know where food and water might be?" asked the little hyenas.

"Well, no," said Big Brother Hyena, "but I'm the biggest, and the baddest, and the best-looking hyena in all the land, which means I must have the biggest brain. So I'll know where to go. Follow me!"

All the little hyenas shrugged their shoulders and said, "Okay."

They followed Big Brother Hyena across the hot, dry land. None of them knew where they were going, including Big Brother Hyena. But nobody questioned his authority. They just kept walking.

The sun was almost noon-high, and the little hyenas were panting and groaning, when Big Brother Hyena noticed a flock of birds overhead. They twittered and chirped about a place where the water was abundant and clean, and the grass grew soft and green, and the trees were filled with fruit.

"Follow me this way!" shouted Big Brother Hyena, as he pointed in the direction the birds flew.

His sisters and brothers and cousins and others said, "Okay."

Soon they came to a place where water rose from underground, creating a pool of clean, clear water, and a fine little river. The grass around the pool and along the banks of the river was thick, soft and green, and the nearby trees were laden with sweet-smelling fruits of every kind.

The little hyenas ran to the water. As they slurped and gulped, Big Brother Hyena sat proudly, and bragged, "See? I told you I'd lead you to food and water." He said nothing about the birds he'd followed to this lovely place.

The little hyenas ate fruit that had dropped into the grass. When their bellies were full, they stretched out in the grass, and went to sleep.

Big Brother Hyena drank, and ate, and sat looking over what he had decided would be his new kingdom. Yes, he would be the king of this place. After all, he was the biggest, and the baddest, and the best-looking hyena in all the land.

The sun settled into a red and orange blanket at the horizon. Big Brother Hyena still sat, proudly surveying his land. Then he saw something slowly climbing above the trees. In the darkening sky, this something rose, big and round and yellowish-white. He'd never seen this thing before. He tried to figure out what it was.

Then Big Brother Hyena called out, "Cheese! There's cheese in the sky! Big and round and yellowish-white cheese!

"I love cheese," Big Brother Hyena said. He reached for the cheese in the sky. He stretched as far as he could, he reached as high as he could, but he couldn't get that big cheese in the sky.

Big Brother Hyena looked around for someone to help him. Asleep in the grass were his sisters and brothers and cousins and others. Big Brother Hyena called to one of his little brothers: "Hey, come here!"

Little Brother Hyena sat up, "Huh?" Then he ran to his big brother, and asked, "Okay, what?"

"Crouch down," said Big Brother Hyena.

Little Brother Hyena said, "Okay, uh, what?"

"I want you to crouch down so that I can climb on your back," said Big Brother Hyena.

"Okay, uh, why?"

"So that I can get that big cheese in the sky," said Big Brother Hyena.

Little Brother Hyena looked toward the sky. There was something round and yellowish-white, rising above the trees. Little Brother Hyena had never noticed it in the night sky.

"Oooh, that's a big cheese!" said Little Brother Hyena. It looked so tasty that he told Big Brother Hyena, "Okay!"

Little Brother Hyena crouched down, and Big Brother Hyena climbed on his back. He stretched as far as he could, he reached as high as he could, but he couldn't reach that big cheese in the sky.

He climbed back down and looked around. There were sisters and brothers and cousins and others still resting in the grass. Big Brother Hyena called out to one of his little sisters, "Hey, come here!"

Little Sister Hyena sat up, "Huh? Then she ran to her big brother, and asked, "Okay, what?"

"I want you to climb on Little Brother Hyena's back," said Big Brother Hyena.

"Okay, uh, why?" asked Little Sister Hyena.

"So I can climb on your back," Said Big Brother Hyena.

"Okay, uh…what?"

"I want you to climb on Little Brother Hyena's back, so that I can climb on your back, so I can reach that big cheese in the sky," explained Big Brother Hyena.

Little Sister Hyena looked toward the sky. There was something round and yellowish-white, rising above the trees. Little Sister Hyena had never noticed it until then.

"Oooh, that's the biggest cheese I ever did see!" giggled Little Sister Hyena. She thought about how good that cheese might taste. She told Big Brother Hyena, "Okay!"

Little Brother Hyena crouched down, and Little Sister Hyena climbed on his back. Then Little Sister Hyena crouched down, and Big Brother Hyena climbed on her back. He stretched as far as he could, he reached as high as he could, but he couldn't reach that big cheese in the sky.

He climbed back down and looked around. There were sisters and brothers and cousins and others still resting in the grass. Big Brother Hyena called out to each of them in turn, "Hey! Hey! Hey! Come here!"

Soon, a column of hyenas wobbled and wibbled in the light of the full moon. On top of all the other hyenas stood Big Brother Hyena. But he couldn't stretch very far, with all those hyenas wobbling underneath him. And he couldn't reach very far, with a fear of falling to the ground making him hold tightly to the hyena beneath him.

How was Big Brother Hyena going to get that big cheese in the sky?

Meanwhile, an old elephant made his way to the pool of clean, clear water. As he sipped and slurped and showered himself, waving his great trunk about, Elephant noticed something strange wibbling and wobbling nearby. It…was…a pile of hyenas!

Elephant walked a little closer to the sight. He called out, "Hey, what you doin'?"

Big Brother Hyena shouted back to him, "Elephant! Come here! I need your help to get that big cheese in the sky!"

Elephant looked cautiously toward the sky. But he didn't see any cheese. He saw the moon.

Elephant said to himself, "That hyena thinks the moon is cheese!" He lifted his trunk and snorted out a laugh.

"Okay, Hyena," said Elephant, "What do you want me to do about it?"

Big brother Hyena shouted, "I have a plan. I want you grab the hyena on the bottom of the pile. I want you to pull him out from the bottom of the pile. Then I want you to throw him to the top of the pile, so that I can climb on his back and reach that big cheese in the sky!"

Elephant couldn't believe what he'd heard. He stretched his ears, and told Big Brother Hyena to repeat what he'd just said. When Elephant heard it the second time, he still couldn't believe it.

"Let me get this straight, "Elephant said. "You want me to grab the hyena on the bottom of the pile…" Elephant started to snicker. "…and pull him out of the pile…" Elephant started to giggle. "and throw him to the top of the pile…" Elephant chuckled. "…so you can climb on his back…" Elephant shook with laughter as he spoke.

" . . . and reach that big . . . cheese . . . in the sky? BWA-HAH-HA . . . . . ."OKAY!"

Elephant stretched out his trunk and grabbed Little Brother Hyena. Then Elephant yanked as hard as he could...yoink! And hyenas began to fall out of the sky.

Each one said the same thing as he or she fell: "AAAAAAAAAH!"

Each one landed hard in the grass and lay upon the ground, including Big Brother Hyena.

"That was funny!" laughed Elephant. "Call me the next time you want to do something that silly. I'll help!" Elephant walked away through the trees, and left the hyenas moaning and groaning in the grass.

Every one of those hyenas had broken back legs, including Little Brother Hyena. They couldn't stand, and they would've died, if the rain hadn't begun to fall.

Rain fell in a soft mist that filled their mouths with sweet water. It soothed their bodies as they lay in the grass, and soothed the dry earth, too. The drought was over.

The hyenas stayed where they were in the rain. After a long, long while, they could stand again.

But their back legs were no longer long and straight and strong. Their legs were bent and their shoulders were slouched, the way a hyena's back legs and shoulders look today, because they carried the burden of someone else's stupidity on their backs.

The hyenas were also bruised with the spots that you see on their shoulders and backs even now, the marks that remind them of a time when they did not think for themselves.

To this day, hyenas laugh. And now you know why. When hyenas laugh, they are remembering this story, and laughing at themselves.

Story Notes

Tales of Hyena are still told in Senegal and the Republic of the Gambia. Tales of Bouki, hyena and trickster, are told from Haiti to Louisiana. I'm not sure where or when my dad might have heard this story, but he told me we had cousins in the West Indies, and that some of his kin had come up from Louisiana "a long time ago". I remember hearing only four or five tales of Hyena when I was very young; I have since found versions of them in collections of Haitian folktales. So I'm guessing this tale of the braggart Big Brother Hyena blossomed from those roots.

Dad's telling of this story didn't include the usual "twang" from his Tennessee and Alabama family ties, but his wording carried a touch of slang and loads of humor. Each character had a voice: Big Brother Hyena was authoritative and proud; Little Brother Hyena was a little shy and confused; Little Sister Hyena squealed and giggled, and spoke with a high, obnoxiously loud pitch. Elephant's trunk apparently gave his speech a throaty, nasal sound; to me, he sounded a lot like Dad's Bear in the Rabbit tales.

If Pop-Pops heard my father telling a hyena tale, he would state (when the story was over, and Dad was out of earshot), "That's not Hyena. That's Fox!" Sometimes he said the protagonist was Wolf. Apparently, Pop-Pops knew similar stories.

Spider and Snake

Spider traipsed through the woods one day, when he heard something rustling and slithering through the grass. Spider looked for it, and oh, how he admired that critter's coat, a coat covered with fine patterns woven of many colors. That coat fit Snake perfectly.

Well, Spider said to Snake, "Man, that's a fine coat. But I would look better in it than you. Why don't you give me that coat?"

Snake said, "Ssspider, you don't need this coat. It'sss not for you. It'sss for me. And, you have thingsss you would never give to me, like the thread you make, and the net you weave with it to catch your food. Would you trade your thread for my coat?"

Spider shook his head, "Oh, no, I wouldn't trade. But, Snake, that coat looks good. Let me borrow it for a while."

Snake shook his head, and slithered farther into the grass. Spider decided he was going to take that coat.

Spider ran to a place where he figured Snake would eventually come. It was a cool, shaded place, near cool stones where Snake could rest. Spider waited there, until he saw the grass moving, and heard the rustling and slithering of someone nearby.

As soon as Spider saw Snake's nose stretching itself out of the grass, Spider fell on his back, and bent up his legs. Then he yelled, "Ow, oh, ow, oh, OW!"

Concerned for Spider's health, Snake slithered closer. He asked, "Brother Ssspider, what'sss wrong with you?"

Spider whimpered, "Oh, some people came along, and just because they didn't like the way I looked, they tried to kill me. They kicked at me, and stomped on me. I think they broke all my legs, see?" Spider bent his legs a little more.

Snake didn't realize that Spider could always bend his legs like that. He felt so sorry for Spider that he offered to do whatever was needed to make him feel better.

"Ssspider, what can I do to help?" he asked.

"Well," said Spider, "I have been traumatized. I believe I'm in shock. I'm feeling weak and sore, and sooo c-c-cold. But I might feel better, if I could have that coat."

Snake offered his coat to Spider. Spider flipped himself right side up, and grabbed Snake's tail. He pulled, while Snake slithered farther and farther out of that fine coat.

When the coat was halfway off his body, Snake asked Spider, "Isss that enough to make you feel better?"

"No, man," said Spider, "I need it ALL!" And Spider snatched off the rest of Snake's coat, and ran with it.

Poor Snake lay naked and cold on the ground, while Spider made his way up a tree, and onto its branch. Spider hung by a thread, up-side down underneath the branch, where he figured no one could reach him. He admired Snake's coat, and started trying it on his own body.

"I will look good in this coat!" Spider bragged.

But the coat lost its wonderful colors. It turned a dull gray, the way a snake's coat does when the snake is no longer in it. Spider didn't want it anymore. He threw it on the ground.

"Hm, I guess I could make a coat of my own. After all, I can spin and weave thread like nobody's business. Why, I'll just make myself a coat, with colors and patterns better than the ones Snake wore," Spider told himself.

But, the thread Spider spun was a dull gray. No matter how hard he tried, he couldn't make it any other color. And he couldn't weave his thread into a coat, either. Some folks say that's because he tricked Snake and stole Snake's fine coat.

And what happened to that poor Snake? Well, after a while, he started growing another coat, with all the fine colors and patterns of the old coat he'd lost. The new coat fit him perfectly.

It's because Snake tried to help Spider, and share his gifts with someone, that snakes can grow new coats today.

Story Notes

Spider in this tale is, for course, Anansi. But in this trickster tale, he doesn't get what he wants. It's nice to have a story in which Snake is not a villain. After all, critters are critters. Only in folktales and fairy tales do they act like people.

Daddy always warned me, "A snake is still a snake. And snakes are trouble." I was a teenager when I finally began to catch on to the fact that he was talking more about people than about snakes.

Daddy said this story was old when he was a baby. His way of putting it was, "This story was old when Methuselah was born." Methuselah was Noah's ancestor in the Bible; he lived to be 969 years old.

That's pretty old, both for a man and for a parable.

The Sing

Rabbit had fallen in love with a sweet little bunny by the name of Miss Molly. Miss Molly was the cutest thing Rabbit had ever seen. Whenever he was around her, Rabbit got all tongue-tied and twisted up inside. He couldn't speak. All he could do was grin, giggle, and look at Miss Molly.

One morning, Rabbit got up the nerve to do a little courting, and to ask Miss Molly's mama for her daughter's hand in marriage. To do that took a lot of courage. Miss Molly's mama was the grandest critter in all the country. She owned the finest house there was and the nicest garden. Hers was better than any two-legged farmer's property. Miss Molly's mama's quilts were so beautiful that folks came from across the country, just to buy one of them. And Miss Molly's mama's pies won the blue ribbon at the county fair every year. Everything about Miss Molly's mama was grand, including her temper.

Well, Rabbit buffed his toenails and cleaned between his teeth with a pine needle. Rabbit brushed his ears and fluffed his tail so he would look good enough to impress Miss Molly's mama.

Then Rabbit took a deep breath and set out for Miss Molly's mama's home.

When Rabbit got to the picket fence around Miss Molly's mama's land, he stopped and looked over the gate. There was Miss Molly, rocking back and forth in the porch swing. She was as cute as clover, and she smiled as warmly and sweetly as a sugar cube melting in cinnamon tea. Seeing her gave Rabbit just enough gumption to open the gate, walk down the brick path, and up the front steps.

There was Miss Molly's mama. Mama was rocking in her favorite rocking chair, and stitching a quilt patch. She looked up at Rabbit and she nodded. That was the signal for Rabbit to sit with Miss Molly.

Mama stayed on the porch, rocking, and stitching. As Rabbit slid into the porch swing next to Miss Molly, Mama kept her eyes on her sewing, but she turned her ears toward the young folks in the porch swing. She listened in on the courtship's proceedings, which was proper.

But all she heard was Rabbit giggling, and her daughter, Molly, giggling. Then Rabbit breathed in, and giggled some more. Molly grinned at him, and she giggled some more. Then Rabbit giggled harder, and Molly giggled louder. After a while, the two lovebirds were cackling like crows, laughing at nothing but love.

This went on and on, until, finally, Miss Molly's Mama yelled, "Shut up!"

Both young lovers stopped their giggling, and looked at Miss Molly's mama to see what was wrong.

"You two act as if you don't have a bit of sense," Miss Molly's mama fussed. "You can't do any courtin' for all the gigglin'!

"Molly, go in the house, and Rabbit, go home, and think of some-thin' to say to my daughter," she continued. "Both of you calm down, and think of somethin' to say. I can't have my daughter actin' so fool-ish that she might marry somebody who doesn't have a brain in his head."

Molly slowly headed for the front door. And Rabbit slowly walked down the front steps. That's when he noticed somebody standing at the front gate, somebody big and strong and mean.

It was Bear.

Bear had come to do a little courting himself. He wasn't in love with anybody; he wasn't even thinking about being in love. It was warm weather season, but Bear knew that winter would come. It always did. Bear was thinking about Miss Molly's mama's nice warm house, so much nicer than a cave. Bear was thinking about Miss Molly's mama's nice warm quilts, so much nicer than a pile of leaves. Bear was thinking about Miss Molly's mama's pies, so much tastier than nuts and berries, especially as the last meal before that long winter's nap.

Bear pushed the front gate open with the force of a storm wind, and stomped down that brick path, cracking the old bricks beneath his big feet. Bear yanked Rabbit up by his ears, and threw him off the porch into the grass. Then, without even a glance at Miss Molly's mama, Bear growled in his low, grumbly voice, "Miss Molly, marry me!"

Miss Molly was speechless. Rabbit was sputtering and stumbling over his own words, too flustered to object. But he leaped up on the porch and stood in front of Miss Molly. For once, he balled up his little fists, ready to fight for the bunny he loved.

"Oh, no!" shouted Miss Molly's mama. "No, no, no, no no!

"I am not gonna have you two fightin' on my front porch! Just stop before you get started. Nobody is courtin' my daughter until I say they can!"

Miss Molly's mama had a temper as big and strong as any bear. Mama set down her quilt patch in the rocking chair. She stood between Rabbit and Bear. She glared at both of them with her mean, beady eyes, and said, "I'm gonna settle this. We are gonna have a sing. You two go off and make up a song, and come back this evening. I'll invite the neighbors and kinfolk over for supper, and then you two will sing your songs. The one that sings the best will have my permission to court my daughter. Now, go!"

Nobody argued with Miss Molly's mama. Molly went in the house. Bear and Rabbit headed for the gate.

Miss Molly's mama crossed her arms in satisfaction. She figured that one of those two boys would have enough brains to make up a good song; if he had a good brain, there was a chance that he'd make a good husband for Molly. And Miss Molly's mama had a notion that she knew which one would win the sing.

All the way down that brick path to the gate, Rabbit muttered to himself. Bear heard Rabbit say, "Well, I could ask Miz Mockingbird to help me with a song. She knows the songs of all the birds. Miz Mockingbird has the most beautiful songs in all the world."

Bear shoved Rabbit out of his way, and made a beeline to Miz Mockingbird's home.

Miz Mockingbird sat in her nest, and rested on three little eggs, until Bear started shaking her tree.

"Oooh," Miz Mockingbird called as she flew down to Bear. "Bear, what do you think you're doing?"

"Miz Mockingbird," said Bear, "Give me a song."

Miz Mockingbird flew around Bear's head, and asked, "What do you mean, give you a song?"

Bear said, "I need a song. Give me one of yours. If you don't, I'll knock down this tree, and I'll eat up your babies. Now, give me a song!"

Miz Mockingbird thought quickly. What could she do to protect her babies, and make this bully go away?

"Ah," she said, "fine. I'll give you a song, but whenever you sing it, you must sing it exactly as I've sung it to you."

Then Miz Mockingbird settled near Bear's ear, and whispered

the song to him, "Tweetly-tweet..."

Bear walked off happy, figuring he had the best song in all the world.

Before Miz Mockingbird could settle herself on those eggs, along came Rabbit.

"Miz Mockingbird," Rabbit called, "Please, Miz Mockingbird, give me a song!"

Miz Mockingbird flew from her nest again. "Rabbit," she squawked, "Why should I give you a song?"

Rabbit sighed, "Because I'm in love. And I have to have the best song in all the world, so that I can ask for Miss Molly's hand in marriage. Please, Miz Mockingbird, will you give me a song?"

"No!' Miz Mockingbird started back to her nest. She gently sat on her eggs, and looked down at Rabbit. "Rabbit, I understand your need, but you can make up a song yourself. Child, you've got a good brain between those ears of yours, and you've had some adventures. You know your stories and the stories of your family. Go home, and make up a song for yourself."

Rabbit said, "Yes, ma'am." He hung his head and sauntered away. But he knew Miz Mockingbird was right. He did have a good brain between his ears.

Well, evening came along wrapped in a soft pink sunset. Miss Molly's mama's kinfolk and neighbors were finishing up the last of the fine vittles she had prepared for them, good things for every kind of critter to eat. With full bellies and satisfied smiles on their faces, they waited for the sing to begin.

Along came Bear, grinning like he'd just finished a fine meal, too. And along came Rabbit, ears down, steps short and trembling.

Before Miss Molly's Mama could choose who would go first, Bear stepped in front of Rabbit and said, "I'm gonna sing first. And I know I'm gonna win, 'cause I stole—uh, got my song from Miz Mockingbird."

Rabbit fretted as Bear cleared his growly throat. This wasn't fair. Bear was supposed to make up the song himself. Rabbit kept thinking about all the beautiful songs Miz Mockingbird knew, and how, now, Bear had one of them.

Bear cleared his throat, "a-heh, a-heh, a-hem." Then he sang the song Miz Mockingbird had whispered to him. Bear sang it exactly the way he heard it:

I'm smart enough to sing this song:

Tweetly-tweet, oo-ee-oo.

Ain't smart enough to know I got it wrong,

Tweetly-tweet, oo-ee-oo.

I'm smart enough to sing these words:

Tweetly-tweet, oo-ee-oo.

But everybody knows I can't sing like a bird,

Tweetly-tweet, oo-ee-oo.

Bear stepped back beside Rabbit, and stood there with a satisfied smile on his face. But he wondered why all the critters in the yard were snickering and giggling and laughing.

Bear went over the song he'd just sung: "I'm smart enough . . . I got it . . . everybody knows I can't sing like a . . . aw, man . . ."

Bear realized what he'd just done. He was so embarrassed, he left the critters still laughing in that yard. Nobody saw him for a long, long time.

Now it was Rabbit's turn to sing. Rabbit stepped forward. He looked at the audience awaiting his performance. He looked at Miss Molly's mama. Then he looked at Miss Molly.

Rabbit took a deep, slow breath, and sang the song he had made up:

My father ate at the garden gate;
my father ate at the garden gate.
The rabbits skip, the rabbits hop,
the rabbits eat up the turnip tops.
U-huh, u-huh, u-huh, yes they do.
Well, my tail is short, but my ears are long;
my tail is short, but my ears are long,
Just like my ma, just like my pa,
just like my dear future mother-in-law...

I guess you now who won the sing.

On the porch that evening, Rabbit sat in the swing right next to Miss Molly. Her mama watched over the proceedings, as was proper. And after the courtship, Rabbit and Miss Molly became husband and wife.

They were married by Reverend Owl in the light of a full moon. And if they didn't live happily ever after, they lived as best they could.

Story Notes

When I was in elementary school, this was as close to a romantic notion as I wanted to get. I remember Daddy telling the story when he and I were on our way home from one of his weekend chores. On Saturday afternoons or Sundays after church, instead of resting from working at two jobs, Daddy did odd jobs for folks who weren't able to do the work for themselves. He cut grass, fixed televisions and radios, weeded gardens and re-hung many a screen door–all in addition to his having tended our yard, visited his relatives to make sure they were okay, and told us bedtime stories on Saturday night.

Most of the time, my mother and my sister and brother didn't seem interested in riding with Daddy to handle these extra duties. Those errands would have meant more work for Ma. And they would have bored my siblings. And Dad tended to make little side-trips whenever he saw a dirt road or an unmarked street. He'd say, "Let's see where this leads." Most of the time those roads led to a place called "Lost." I think everybody else in the family got tired of visiting "Lost."

But I liked the adventure of it. And on the way to or from "Lost," Daddy told stories.

I liked the imagery of Rabbit using his head to defeat a bully and win the hand of his beloved. Using the "good brain" between his ears was what Rabbit did all the time. I hoped I had a good brain between my ears, too.

Calling Miss Molly's mama just that, instead of giving her a name, seemed to fit Daddy's ways. Daddy always wanted to know folks, and he surely wanted me to show respect for elders. He didn't have to know an elder's name in order to be respectful. A full-grown man, he still said, "Yes, ma'am" and "No, sir" to folks older than he. He expected us to do the same.

There's an old wedding superstition in this tale. A full moon on or near the day of one's wedding is supposed to be good luck, and a promise of a bountiful life together.

The ending was my favorite part. I remember the tune for the songs, and I still use it in my own storytelling; it's almost the same for both Bear's and Rabbit's singing, but Bear uses a low, deep, goofy kind of voice (similar to Elephant's in "Hyena and the Big Cheese"), and Rabbit taps his foot and slaps his leg as he sings a much better version. But the singing wasn't as special as that last line—we don't all get to "happily ever after", but we can all aspire to living as best we can.

Folks

Our family's folktales are largely populated with critters of the four-legged, winged, and occasionally finned variety, but a small number of two-legged folks walk along the paths of a few tales. Some of them have names like John or Sarah Mae, but some are nameless—"that girl, "a young man", "an old man and an old woman"; their genealogy can be traced to the British Isles, to the hero of the beanstalk story and the fool tales in which someone who was called "clever" probably wasn't. A few stories of these women and men, or their children and grandchildren, remain in my memory and come to life in my storytelling.

Three Suitors

Once there was a young woman who lived with her family in the finest house in all the county. The house sat on a hill overlooking the family property, fields of wheat and corn in their season, and orchards of apples, cherries, and pears, gardens of vegetables, and meadows where the cows, the horses, and the chickens roamed freely. That girl's family was the wealthiest in the community, and she had reached the age where she was expected to marry.

That was good news to the young men. Some of them planned to do a little courting.

One sunny afternoon, as that girl sat on the front porch with her mama and Daddy, she heard the sound of a wagon coming up the road to their house. A young man held the reins to the horse that pulled that wagon. When he got close to the house, the young man stopped that horse, jumped down from the wagon, and pulled two big axes from it.

He was good-looking and strong. He stomped toward the house, and swung those axes into the first step to the porch, k-cha! Then he grinned at that young woman, and said, "Baby-cakes, marry me."

Her mama was sputtering, "You, y-you, you just knocked holes in our porch step with those axes! W-why did you do that?"

"Why, I've come to ask for your daughter's hand in marriage," said that young man. He grinned even wider as he held out his hand toward the daughter of the household and again said, "Baby-cakes, marry me."

Well, that girl's daddy nearly had a fit. But the girl said, "Mama,

Daddy, go in the house. I'll take care of this myself."

Mama and Daddy went in the house, but they stood at the screen door and listened.

"So, you want me to marry you," said their daughter. "Why should I do that?"

"Why? Well, I am the best woodsman in all the land. I can cut wood faster than anybody, and make the finest furniture you ever did see. You could do no better for a husband. You should marry me," said the young man.

He smiled with confidence, but the young woman didn't seem impressed. That young man tried to think of a way to show her what a good catch he was.

He pulled his axes out of the broken wood of the porch step, and headed for the tallest tree in the front yard. He swung his axes, k-cha, into its trunk, and pulled himself up the trunk using only those axes.

When he got to the top, he started swinging those axes. Wood flew as he chopped and fell, stripping the bark and shaping each piece on its way to the ground. The wood fell in the shape of a huge chair, and the young man, axes in hand, fell into its seat with a thud.

Again, he grinned at that young woman.

She said, "I have no words to say to you right now. But if you come to the dance at the meeting house on Friday evening, I'll meet you there at 7 P.M., and I'll have something to say to you then."

Satisfied with himself, the young woodsman made his way to his wagon, threw the axes into its bed, jumped up into the seat, and set his horse to pulling the wagon back down the road.

He passed a sporty car making its way up the road. It was driven by a handsome young man in a fine suit. That young man stopped the car in the front yard, and jumped out right in front of the young woman.

He was shiny from his slick hair to his patent leather shoes. He wore a silk suit, silk shirt, silk tie, and a slick smile, teeth so white that the sun glinted off them.

He reached out for that girl's hand, and said, "Honey, marry me."

That girl could hear her parents stammering and sputtering behind the front door screen. But she figured she could handle this herself.

"Why should I marry you," she asked that shiny young man.

"Don't you know who I am?" he asked. "My family is the second wealthiest in the county, almost as wealthy as yours. If you and I married, we'd be the richest couple in the state!

"I'm also a landowner. I buy and sell land and make a lot of money for myself. And I know how to build houses, too," bragged the shiny young man.

The young woman didn't seem impressed. You know that shiny young man wanted to impress her.

He looked around the front yard, and saw a big wooden chair. He went to his car, pulled a tool box from its trunk, walked over to that chair, and tore it apart. Then, with saw and sander, with hammer and nails, he turned what had been a chair into a fine little house.

Well, that girl still didn't seem impressed, but the family dog yelped with joy, ran from under the front porch, and moved right into that house.

The young woman sighed. She said, "I have no words to say to you right now. But if you come to the dance at the meeting house on Friday evening, I'll meet you there at 7 P.M., and I'll have something to say to you then."

That made the shiny young landowner sparkle and smile. He put his tools back in their box, set the tool box in the trunk, slammed the trunk shut, jumped into the driver's seat, and zoomed down the road.

He passed a young man on a big white horse. The horse clippety-clopped up the hill, lickety-split, until its rider stopped it in the front yard and tied its reins to the roof of a big doghouse.

The rider swung his long legs over the side of the horse, then swung his long jacket away from his sides as he set his fists on his waist, and proudly announced, "I have come to ask for your hand in marriage. Sweetie-pie, marry me."

As he held out his hand to the young woman who stood frowning in front of him, he thought he heard gagging sounds from behind the house's screened front door.

She knew her parents were going apoplectic, but the girl figured she could handle this situation herself.

She folded her arms as she asked, "Now, why do you think I should marry you?"

The young man smoothed his perfectly coifed hair, and said, "I am the best barber in all the land. That might not sound like much to you, but I can tell you it pays me well enough to someday get me out of this little country town.

"I have trimmed the mustaches and shaved the beards of very influential people. Politicians come all the way from Washington DC to have me cut their hair. There's one senator, doesn't even have hair, comes down here for me to polish his head once a month. One day, honey, I'll take you away to a big city, maybe Washington DC, if you marry me."

That young woman didn't seem impressed. The young barber was trying to find a way to gain her interest, when a rabbit hopped out of the bushes and into the front yard. The family dog shot out of that house in the front yard, and started chasing that rabbit hither and yon.

That gave the young barber an idea.

He reached into one pocket of his long jacket, and pulled out a shaving mug, a mug brush, and soap. He spit into the mug, stirred around the soap in there, put the brush into his pocket, and pulled out a razor. He snapped that razor open, and watched for that rabbit to come close.

As the rabbit ran past him, that barber snatched up the critter, and proceeded to lather him up and shave him clean from the tips of his bunny ears to the toes on each little paw. Then the barber dropped that poor rabbit on the ground, where it stood stiff, still, and naked of its fur.

The rabbit looked a bit confused. The dog, running up on that poor critter, was even more confused. It sure didn't look like a rabbit.

The dog yelped, whimpered, and ran into his new house. The rabbit just sat on the ground, looking confused.

The barber looked pleased. He smiled at that young woman. She looked just as confused as that rabbit.

"You just shaved a rabbit!" she cried. "And I have no words to say to you right now. But if you come to the dance at the meeting house on Friday evening, I'll meet you there at 7 P.M., and I'll have something to say to you then."

The barber slipped his equipment back into his long pockets, got on his horse, and rode away.

Well, Friday evening found three young men dressed in their finest clothes and standing at the door of the community meeting house. Each one wondered why the other two were there.

At 7 PM on the dot, that young woman came to the door with Mama and Daddy. Her parents passed those young men with not so much as a nod or greeting, and the young woman stood before them.

Each young man held his hand out to that girl, and realized why the other two men were standing there.

The young woman straightened herself until she stood as tall as she could, and she said, "I tried to think of what I might say to all of you, and I think the simplest thing I can say is, no, I will not marry any one of you. But maybe I should tell you why.

"You, mister woodsman, cut down the oldest, finest tree on our property. It was planted by one of our ancestors a long time ago, and grew and stood strong, until you cut it down and turned it into a chair in our front yard. But not once did you act as if you'd pull me on your lap in that chair, and act as if you loved me.

"You, mister landowner, tore down a perfectly good chair and turned it into a house we did not need in the front yard. Now, the dog lives there instead of in his nice little house in the backyard. You built a house, but not once did you act as if you loved me and would make a home with me.

You, mister barber, …you shaved a rabbit! I don't know what to say about that!"

The young men shuffled nervously, but that young woman wasn't finished.

"Besides all that," she went on, "You all acted as if you were hungry for something—'Baby-cakes', 'Honey', 'Sweetie-pie'—but it sure didn't feel like you were hungry for my love. Not one of you called me by my name. By the way, it's 'Katherine'.

"The next time you decide to do a little courting, it might be good to remember to call a woman by her name."

The young woman went into the dance, and had a good time with her family and friends. The three young men went home, a bit sadder, and a bit wiser than they'd been.

When the dance was over, that young woman went on home with her family. Whether she married or not, I was never told. But because she could handle things herself, she lived happily ever after.

Story Notes

I remember Pop-Pops telling this story, and making the motions of shaving a rabbit—that was my favorite part. I was approaching an age when young men were smiling at me, and I was smiling back.

The story seems timeless. One young man guides a wagon, one drives a car, one rides a horse. No date or decade was given for the origins of the story, but I always envisioned the young woman in a long dress, sitting in a porch swing, sipping lemonade with her family at a Victorian home. Ah, the imagination of a girl on the verge of womanhood can create romantic visions, even when a story's romance is dashed by a chair, a dog house, and a naked rabbit!

Oh, John, No!

One morning, John went to his mama and announced, "Mama, I've learned all I need to learn. I'm goin' out to make my own way in the world."

"Oh, John, no," said Mama. "You don't know enough to make your own way in the world, not yet. Why, you don't know what goes on right here on the farm. You don't even know what goes on in our barn. You can't possibly be ready to go out into the world."

John insisted, "Mama, I know enough. I've read, uh...three big books. I don't need to learn anymore. I am goin' out to make my own way in the world."

"Fine," said Mama. "You go, but remember, times are hard and folks are troubled. They're struggling to find work and feed their families. If you see folks workin', that's a good thing. You greet those folks, you say hello. You tell 'em, 'may you always have plenty of work to do, and plenty to fill your mouth, too'."

John said, "Yes, ma'am, I'll remember that. And now, I'm goin' out to make my way in the world."

John walked out the door and down the sidewalk, through the gate, all the way to the barn.

When he got close to the barn, he remembered what his mama had said. He really didn't know much about what happened on their farm, didn't even know what went on in the barn. So he looked in there to see what was going on.

Some men were working in there, cleaning out all the dirty stuff that can settle on the floor of a barn. They were shoveling out the stinky stuff that horses do, and the stinky stuff that goats do, and the stinky stuff that chickens do on the floor of a barn.

John remembered what his mama had told him. He said, "Hi! May you always have plenty of that to do, and plenty for your mouth, too!"

Well, those men stopped working. They looked at John. One of them asked, "What did you say?"

John said, "I said, 'Hi! May you always have plenty of that to do, and plenty for your mouth, too'!"

That man looked at John, looked at what was in his shovel, looked at John, and threw what was in the shovel at John.

John went running for the gate, through the gate, up the sidewalk, through the door into the house. He shouted, "Mama! Somebody is throwin' stinky stuff on a poor little fella!"

Mama came, calling out, "What's that you say, John? What stinky stuff, what…eeeew, John!"

Mama drew a bath for John, filled the tub with warm water and bubbly soap, got him some clean towels and clean clothes. She sat near the bathroom door while John cleaned himself up, and she asked him what he'd seen and said and done.

John told her.

Mama said, "Oh, John, no. You shouldn't have said what you said to those men. They're doing hard work nobody else wants to do. You should've praised them. You should've said somethin' like, 'Good job, well done'."

By that time, John was bathed and dressed. He came out the bathroom and said, "I'll remember that, Mama. And now, I'm goin' out to make my way in the world."

John walked out the door and down the sidewalk, through the

gate, quickly past the barn, and down the road to town. He saw someone walking toward him.

It was a bunch of folks all dressed in black. Some were moaning and some were crying and some were shaking their heads in sorrow as they walked behind six strong men who carried a long wooden box on their shoulders.

John remembered what his mama had told him. He stepped off the road as the funeral procession approached, and shouted, "Good job! Well done!"

That whole funeral procession stopped. The six strong men gently set the box on the road. One of them walked up to John and asked, "What did you just say?"

John smiled and said, "I said 'Good job! Well done!'"

That man wasn't sure what John meant by that, but it didn't seem like the right thing to say. He shook John by his shoulders, until John's eyeballs were rolling around in his head.

When the man let go, John ran up the road. He passed the barn, ran through the gate, up the sidewalk, and through the front door.

John shouted, "Mama! Somebody is shakin' a poor little fella until his eyeballs are rollin' around in his head!"

Mama came, looked at John, and asked, "Oh, John, why are your eyeballs rollin' around like that?"

She got some cold water at the well, dipped a rag into a bucket of that cold water, slapped that rag on John's eyeballs, and hoped they'd straighen themselves out. While John patted his eyeballs with that rag, Mama asked him what he'd seen and said and done.

John told her.

"Oh, John, no!" Mama cried. "That's not what you should've said. That was a funeral procession, a sad occasion. Those folks were head-in' for the cemetery about to bury somebody! Why, you should've wrung your hands together in sorrow and said something like, 'oh, how sad, this is terrible may your sorrow end soon'."

By that time, John's eyeballs had straightened out. John handed the rag to his mama and said, "Yes, ma'am, I'll remember that. And now, I'm going out to make my way in the world."

John walked out the door and down the sidewalk, through the gate and quickly past the barn, and down the road to town. He heard someone coming up behind him.

John stepped off the road for another procession. A crowd of people ran alongside a little wagon pulled by two white horses. The horses' manes and tails were decorated with ribbons and flowers. People laughed as they carried baskets filled with flower petals, pretty petals that they tossed at the young couple in the wagon. The young man, dressed in a crisp, white shirt, proudly held the reins and gazed lovingly at the young woman beside him. She was a picture of beauty and love, all dressed in a pretty white gown, and her hands were filled with a bright bouquet of flowers.

As the wedding headed to town, John remembered what his Mama had told him. He wrung his hands and shouted, "Oh, how sad! This is terrible! May your sorrow end soon!"

Everybody stopped. The bride started to cry. The groom brought the wagon to a halt. He jumped down from the wagon, and glared at John.

"What did you say?" the groom asked John.

John said, "I said 'Oh, how sad. This is terrible. May your sorrow end soon'."

The groom grabbed the bride's bouquet from her hands, and threw it at John.

Flowers went up John's nose and down his shirt, in his ears and into his hair. John ran up the road. He passed the barn, ran through the gate, and in the front door.

"Mama!" John shouted, "Somebody's throwin' flowers up a poor little fella's nose!"

Mama came, but she didn't seem to move as quickly as she had the first two times. She looked at John for a while before she said, "John, you have flowers stickin' outta your nose."

Mama pulled flowers out of John's nose, his ears, his shirt, and his hair. Then she asked him what he'd seen and said and done.

John told her.

"Oh, John, no!" Mama shouted. "John, that was a wedding procession, a happy occasion! You never should've said that to the bride and groom! You should've pulled out that little flute you keep in your back pocket, and tweedled a happy tune for the newlyweds. You should've run back and forth and shouted hooray and hurrah for them!"

"Yes, ma'am, I'll remember that," said John as he wiped his nose on his arm. "And now, I'm still goin' out to make my way in the world!"

John walked out the door and down the sidewalk, through the gate, quickly past the barn, and down the road, down the road, down the road to town.

At the edge of town, John heard a great commotion. He saw folks running to the nearby duck pond; they carried buckets and pots and pans, filled them with water, and ran to a little house whose porch steps had somehow caught fire. A little old woman jumped up and down near the house. She screamed, "My house, my house! Do something!" as folks dumped water on her porch steps.

John did something. He remembered what his mama had told him.

John pulled his little flute out of his back pocket, and put it to his lips. He tweedled a happy little tune, then ran back and forth and shouted, "Hooray! Hurrah!"

That little old woman hobbled over to John, and asked, "W-w-what did you say?"

John played his flute again, and said, "I said 'hurray, hurrah!'."

The old woman picked up an empty bucket, and pushed it down right over John's head.

John couldn't see a thing, but he ran back up the road, ran right into a tree, but he kept on going. He ran past the barn, and right into the gate, but he kept on going. He ran up the sidewalk, and into the front door, but he kept on going until he was in the house.

There, John shouted, "BABA, SUBBUDDY IS THROWIN' A BUCK-ET OBER A POOR LIDDLE PELLA'S HEAD!"

Mama took her time coming toward the door, until she saw John with a bucket on his head. "John!" she shouted, and she shoved John to his knees, grabbed that bucket, and pulled and pulled until it slid and popped off John's head.

"Ow," said John.

Mama asked him what he'd seen and said and done.

John told her.

"Oh, John, no!" Mama moaned. "That old woman's house was burnin', and you were cheering for the fire!"

Mama was ready to cry, but she tried to give John a little advice, again. She took a deep breath, and said, "John, when you see a fire, you yell, 'FIRE!', so folks come runnin' to help put it out. Then you run for water yourself, you gather up as much water as you can, and you throw it on the fire."

Mama sighed, and said, "John, do you understand?"

John sighed, too. He said, "Yes, ma'am, Mama, I understand. And now, I'm still goin' out to make my own way in the world!"

And John walked out the door and down the sidewalk, through the gate and quickly past the barn, and down the road, down the road, down the road again.

By that time, the fire was out. It had just singed the old woman's front steps a bit. John wasn't sure how such a thing might happen, but he didn't think on it too long, for there was a commotion coming from the center of town.

John ran to see what was afoot. There, in the town square, people were dancing to the music of a fine band. Among the dancers were the bride and groom and the whole wedding party. Around the border of the square, tables had been set up and covered with white tablecloths. Some folks were feeding their faces with the delicious treats on every table, while others clapped their hands or took partners for the dance.

It was a grand celebration. And in the middle of it all, some older gentlemen kept their eyes on half a cow, turning on a spit, over a great, big...

"FIRE!" John yelled, for he remembered what his mama had told him. "FIRE!" he yelled again as he ran for the duck pond. There were buckets still set beside the pond. John filled one to the brim, ran back to the party, and put out the fire.

Not long after that, Mama heard John walk into the house. He sounded kind of squishy.

Mama slowly walked into the front hall, and there was John.

He was drenched from head to toe, as if somebody had thrown

a poor little fella into the duck pond.

Mama shook her head. "John," she said, "I don't want to hear what you saw or said or did. You just listen to me. You have not learned enough to make your way out in the world. You need to stay here and learn more from the books on the shelves, and your studies in school, and life on this farm.

"Do you understand, John?"

John said, "Yes, ma'am." And he didn't say anything else.

He stayed at home until he'd learned a good bit more, and when he finally went out in the world, let's hope he lived the way some folks do at the end of these kinds of stories…

…happily ever after.

Story Notes

This is one of the few tales that I remember having that "happily ever after" ending tacked on to it. I reminded Pop-Pops that my daddy said folks lived "as best they could". Pop-Pops told me, "When your daddy tells the story, he can end it any way he wants, Knot-head."

I think that was the reason for my grandfather telling the tale. "Knot-head" was a nickname I'd earned for being stubborn. I'd heard it so much that I thought it was part of my real name, and informed my kindergarten teacher that she had left it out when she took attendance.

Then I learned the nickname meant I was stubborn. Seems like that was a family trait. It took a long time for some folks to let go of a notion, even when that notion caused problems in their lives or threatened their well-being. For the longest time, I was a child who said, "Yes, ma'am, but…"

"Yes, ma'am" would have been sufficient. But if I'd been the kind of child who simply said "yes, ma'am", I might not have heard this story.

No Fishin' on Sunday

An old man and an old woman lived together in an old house near the crik*. The old woman liked to spend her time in church. The old man liked to go fishing.

It was Sunday morning. The old woman got herself ready for church. The old man got himself ready to fish. He picked up his fishing pole, and said, "Goodbye."

The old woman said, "You should be goin' to church. This is a holy day. No fishin' on Sunday."

The old man said, "This is a holy day, and I remember a story of the loaves and fishes. I'm goin' fishin'. I'll get the loaves at supper."

Out he went, while his wife fussed and hollered, "No fishin' on Sunday!"

The old man made his way to the river. The old woman made her way to church. That was that.

But the old man really wasn't worried about catching any fish. He carried no bait, and no hook, not even a basket to carry back some fish. He was planning on taking a nice Sunday morning nap down by the crik.

The old man found a fine place for a nap, a shady spot underneath a willow tree, where nobody would see him. He sat under that tree, and threw out his hookless, baitless line on the water. He hugged the fishing pole between his knees, leaned back against that tree, and went to sleep.

Imagine his surprise when he felt a tug on the line. The old man sat up in time to see a big fish walking on his tail, coming right out of the water. That big fish held the line in one of his fins as he waddled up to the man.

"Well, well," said the old man. "What am I gonna do with a fish like you?"

"Take me home," said the fish.

"I can't carry you home," said the old man. "You're a big'un, too big to carry. How am I gonna get you home?"

The fish held the line underneath his fin. "Walk me home," said the fish.

The old man held his fishing pole, and led that big fish home. But when he got there, he wasn't sure what to do next.

"I've never had to deal with a fish like you. I'm not sure what I'm supposed to do," said the old man.

The fish dropped the line, and waddled into the house. "Cook me," said the fish.

"But I don't know how to cook such a thing as you," said the old man. So the fish knocked open a cupboard, grabbed a skillet with his fins, tossed it onto the cook stove, got the flames goin'. Then he flipped the can of bacon grease so that it spilled and greased that skillet. The fish knocked over the cornmeal tin, rolled around in the spilled cornmeal, salted and peppered himself up, and threw himself into the skillet.

"Well, I've never seen anything like that happen," said the old man. "What could happen next?"

The cooked fish jumped off the skillet, set the table with a plate, a knife and a fork. Then he grabbed a napkin from the sideboard and tied it around the old man's neck. He shoved the old man into his chair, and jumped onto the plate.

"Eat me," said the fish.

"Uh, I don't think I can. Why, I don't think I should! I..."

The old man didn't get to finish what he was saying. That fish jumped into his mouth and wriggled down his throat.

Oh, that old man felt sick! He could feel that fish wiggling around in his belly.

"Oh, no! Now, what am I gonna do?" moaned the old man.

"Go back to the crik," said the fish in his belly

The old man slowly rose from his chair, and headed for the crik. He had never felt so poorly. The fish wiggled and wobbled inside him, and slapped its tail against the sides of his belly.

When the old man finally got to the crik, he just fell on the ground under that willow tree and cried, "Oh, Lord, what am I gonna do?"

The fish jumped out of his mouth, and said, "Go to church. No fishin' on Sunday."

Then that big fish waddled back into the crik and disappeared.

That old man ran back home, changed into his Sunday-go-to-meetin' clothes, and shot down the road to church.

He slid into the pew next to his wife, and folded his hands in prayer.

The old woman couldn't believe her eyes! She whispered, "What are you doin' here? I thought you were goin' fishin'!"

Sh," whispered the old man, "we're in church. No fishin' on Sunday!"

*A "crik" is a creek. We also knew of "hollers", which were naturally hollowed-out places such as small valleys, and "hills", which were actually the Appalachian foothills.

Story Notes

Pop-Pops told this story. Sometimes he sang the fish's words. And sometimes, the fish popped out of the old man's belly-button, then picked up the belly button and put it back in place.

Of course, this was an admonition to attend church. Funny thing, Pop-Pops never missed church on Sunday, but sometimes he went "fishin", and returned with jars of a clear liquid he called his "special water". Pop-Pops never brought that "special water" to the supper table. He kept his private stock in a cupboard in the cellar, and drank it with his friends on the back porch, as if to hide it from Grandma Jo and the other women in the family, who disapproved of what they knew was in Pop-pops' glass.

Sistah Sarah Mae

Sarah Mae was the prettiest young woman in all the countryside, but she didn't intend to stay in the country forever. She was the only child of a wealthy farm family that had given her everything she'd ever wanted: fine dresses, fancy shoes, and lessons in manners and proper ways. But Sarah Mae wanted to get away from her folks, who gave her the nickname, "Sistah."

She wanted to leave her family's rich farmland and simple life, to get away from the country life and move to a big city.

Every day, a young man from the farm just on the other side of their own would walk past Sistah Sarah Mae's house, and try to find a reason to stop and talk with her. There she'd be, sitting on the front porch or on the window seat in the parlor. She smelled of rose or lilac water. She pinched her cheeks and bit her lips to make them pink. She made sure her hair was perfect, smoothed her dress, and posed at the window or on the front porch. She waited for a fine young man to walk down the road from that big city folks said was over six hills and around seven curves in the road.

Sarah Mae would stare down that road, and dream of a rich life in that big city somewhere beyond the hills.

The young man from the farm next door tried to speak to her, but Sarah Mae turned up her nose, and looked away. The young man bowed his head, and went on to whatever he needed to do. And Sarah Mae sat, prim and pretty, waiting for a young man from the city to come her way.

One morning, as Sarah Mae sat at the window, she saw a handsome young man walking down that road. He was perfect, and perfectly dressed, and he seemed to glide toward her front steps.

Sarah Mae bit her lips and pinched her cheeks, smoothed her dress and patted her hair, fixed the buckles on her red velvet shoes, and posed in the window, ready for that handsome young man to come to the door, and ask to do a little courting.

He didn't. When he got to the turn in the road, the handsome young man headed for the woods.

Sistah Sarah Mae couldn't believe she'd been ignored. She ran out on the porch, and cleared her throat, but the young man didn't turn back toward her.

Sarah Mae ran off the porch, and started following that handsome young man.

His back looked as good as his front, perfectly dressed and moving in such a perfect way.

"Excuse me," Sarah Mae said. "Hello, my name is Sarah Mae. Folks around here call me 'Sistah'."

That handsome young man didn't look back at her. He just kept on moving toward the woods.

"I live in that big house back there at the crossroads. Would you like to come on back and sit on the porch with me, maybe have something cool to drink?"

The young man seemed to take no notice of Sarah Mae. This frustrated her to no end.

"Apparently you don't know who I am. My father has the biggest farm in three counties. Lots of young men consider me a catch. They would love to make me their wife. Wouldn't you like to stop and talk with me a while?"

The young man never turned his head. He kept moving, but he

said, "Young woman, you would do well not to follow me."

Well, he looked too good for Sarah Mae to let him get away. "You can call me 'Sistah'," she said. "Everybody around her calls me that." She chattered on and on, as the two of them approached the woods.

Then that young man's arms fell off.

Sarah Mae looked at the arms lying in the road. She wasn't sure what to say.

"Uh, excuse me," Sarah Mae said, "I don't want to alarm you, but your arms just fell off."

That young man just kept on moving. "I have no need for armsss," he said, "and Sssissstah, you would do well not to follow me."

Well, even without his arms, that young man looked good. Sarah Mae kept on following him and trying to start a conversation.

Then that young man's leg fell off.

Sarah Mae tried to be polite. "Excuse me," she said, "but your leg just fell off, too."

The young man just kept moving. "I have no need for legsss," he said, "and Sssissstah, you would do well not to follow me."

Well, even with his arms gone and one leg on the ground, that young man still looked good to Sarah Mae. She kept on following him.

The sun seemed to disappear as the two made their way in to the woods. Things were quiet there, except for the sound of the birds and bugs, and Sarah Mae, still blathering on.

They reached a place where the shadows were almost as dark as evening's shade. Under a big black walnut tree, the young man turned to Sistah Sarah Mae. He shrugged, and slid out of that one shoe, and the suit fell from his body. He shrugged again, and his mask, with the perfect hair still attached, fell from his face.

"I told you not to follow me. I had no need for armsss or legsss. And I did not come down that road looking for a mate. I came in sssearch of a meal."

He rose above Sistah Sarah Mae, and stared at her with his golden eyes, the biggest snake anyone had ever seen.

That big snake opened his mouth, let his jaw drop, and started slurping down Sistah Sarah Mae. Then he fell to the ground, his belly too full for digesting her. You could hear Sarah Mae's muffled cries coming from that snake. You could see Sarah Mae's little red velvet shoes, kicking out of his mouth.

Well, it just so happened that the young farmer from next door was bringing some firewood home to his ma and Pa. He heard something muffled and low, a cry, as if somebody needed help.

The young farmer dropped his firewood, and ran in the direction of the sound. In the shadows under a big black walnut tree, he saw what looked like a huge log, but it was moving.

Then he saw a pair of red velvet shoes, kicking out of one end of that thing.

"S-sistah Sarah Me?" he asked, "Is that you?"

"M-m-melp!" cried Sarah Mae. "M-m-met m-me out!"

That young farmer grabbed Sarah Mae's feet and he pulled, and pulled, and pulled, until that girl popped out of that big snake's mouth.

Nobody had ever stolen a meal right out of him. That big snake slithered off, and disappeared from those parts.

And there stood Sarah Mae. She was covered from head to toe in the belly slime of a snake. She snorted and sniffed, said, "Thank you" to that young man.

"You saved my life," she said through the slobber and drool.

"Would you like to come home with me and do a little courtin'?

"No, thank you very much," said the young farmer. "You don't look the way you used to, and you definitely don't smell the way you used to, and there's something else. While you were turnin' your nose up at me, the young woman from the farm on the other side of our property started invitin' me over. She learned how to make my favorite pie, and we've been doing a little courtin'," so I don't want to marry you anymore.

"But," the young farmer continued, "I will take you home, if you walk about six feet behind me—peee-yew!"

Well, you'd think after an adventure like that, Sistah Sarah Mae would've changed her ways.

Nope. The next day, she was sitting at the window again, dressed in her finest clothes and shoes, her cheeks pinched and her lips pursed and every hair in place as she waited for a rich and handsome young man to come down the road from the city.

And, unless she died, she's still sitting and waiting.

Story Notes

This was obviously a cautionary tale, told with horrid sound effects and visual imagery that still remains in my memory. Daddy wanted to make sure I knew that looks, money, and an upscale life weren't everything.

I figured this was a good story to end these tales of the two-legged, the "folks" in my family's folktales.

It's also a good point to begin the next section.

Spookers & Haints

Some of my favorite tales were the kind that might keep me up at night. They were sometimes silly, and sometimes frightening, but always awe-inspiring.

The term "haint" is apparently a regional one. From my own travels and conversations, I have found that the word is spoken and understood by folks from West Virginia to Florida, and in the states along the Gulf of Mexico through Texas. When I use it just about anywhere else, somebody asks, "Do you mean 'haunt'?"

Of course this "thang" is a "haunt", a lost and drifting spirit or soul. But most haints are angry, or vengeful, or at least a bit mischievous and ornery. They live in cabins in the woods, or old houses on hills or in swampy valleys, nothing as fine as a mansion, unless it's been abandoned and left to fall into ruin.

"Haunt" is just too proper a word for them.

"Spookers" are creatures in the shadows, but they're not necessarily dead. They are the thing you might see from the corner of your eye., the dead thing revived and walking or sitting where it might torment you, the monster that creeps up the stairs or waits at the foot of the bed. They are thangs, haints, boo hags, big boo daddies, little boo babies, monsters, ghosts...there were so many of these creatures in my daddy's stories that I grew up unafraid of such things., because I knew them. I'd already met them in stories.

As my great-grandmother, Essie Arkward, said, "Dead folks don't bother you much. It's the living folks you have to worry about."

No, I'm Not!

Old man sat on his porch every day, but he never talked to anybody. He just sat there, frowning at the passersby, never having a kind word for anyone.

Well, he got sick. And neighbors being neighbors, when they didn't see the old man out on the porch, they knocked on the door and found him sick in his bed, and they sent some neighbor for the doctor.

When the Doctor came to the old man's bedside, the old man saw the young doctor standin' there. The old man scowled and said, "What you doin' here?"

Doctor said, "Neighbors called me because you're sick. You're very sick."

"No, I'm not!" fussed the old man. "Go away!" So the doctor and the neighbors went away.

But the next day, doctors being doctors, the young doctor came back to check on the old man. Old man was in worse shape than he'd been in the day before. So the young doctor sent some neighbor for the old preacher.

The preacher came to the old man's bedside. Old man saw the old preacher and the young doctor standin' there. Old man said, "What you doin' here?"

The doctor said, "You're very sick."

Old man said, "No, I'm not!"

Old preacher said, "You are very sick. Doctor sent for me, because you are goin' to die."

Old man said, "No, I'm not. Go away!"

So the doctor and the preacher and the neighbors went away.

But the next day, well, you know, doctors bein' doctors, and preachers bein' preachers, and neighbors bein' neighbors, they all came back to check on the old man.

He was dead.

It was a hot day and there was nobody who could preserve that body. Right away, some folks got to buildin' a coffin, and some folks got to diggin' a hole at the cemetery down the road. The men who knew that old man the best laid him out on a tablecloth on his kitchen table. And they wrapped him in that tablecloth, and lifted him out through the back window, and laid him in the coffin.

Preacher said a few words and men nailed the lid onto that coffin. Folks carried the coffin; the preacher walking behind it. The whole procession of folks sang hymns all the way to the cemetery. Then the preacher said some more words, prayers were lifted, and the coffin was lowered into the ground. Preacher tossed a handful of dirt on the coffin. Folks prayed while the shovels worked the buryin'.

Then everybody went home.

Well, the village folks figured they'd tend to what needed to be done after that, the cleanin' out of the house, and the sellin' of the property, since there wasn't much value to any of it, and, as far as folks knew, weren't any relatives. The next day, two of the womenfolk in that little village set out to do the cleanin' part, to pack clothes and dishes for givin' away or for tradin', or sellin' to touristy folk.

When they got to the porch, there was that old man, sittin' in his chair. Graveyard dirt rested around his feet. The tablecloth that had been his shroud was wrapped over his legs like a blanket. He frowned at those women, and said, "What you doin' here?"

Well, those women got to screaming, "What are we doin' here??? What are you doin' here? You're dead!"

Old man leaned on back in his chair, said, "No, I'm not!"

"But we buried you yesterday evenin'!"

"Maybe you were a bit too quick on that," said the old man. "I'm not dead. Can't be dead. Won't believe I'm dead until somebody proves it. Now, go away!"

And the old man just sat there, scowling as mean and ornery as ever.

The women hiked up their skirts and ran for the doctor. He came back with the women. By that time, the old man was startin' to smell a bit. The doctor checked the old man's heartbeat, his pulse, and his breathin'. There wasn't any. Doctor said, "Sir, you should be in your grave. You're dead!"

"No, I'm not!" said the old man. "I'm not dead. Can't be dead. Won't believe I'm dead until somebody proves it. Now, go away!"

The doctor and the two women ran for the preacher. He came back with them. By that time, the old man was startin' to smell a bit worse. The preacher and the doctor checked for breath, and heartbeat, and pulse again, noticed the old man was kind of stiff in that chair. The doctor lifted up the old man's arm, to check his pulse at the wrist again, and that arm snapped and broke and hung kind of funny at the elbow.

Well, the preacher got skitterish then, jumped off the porch, wavin' his Bible over his head, and prayin' loud and hard, and tellin' the old man to go back to the cemetery.

Old man said, "Ain't' no use making all that noise. I'm not goin' anywhere."

"But, man, you're dead!" cried the preacher. And the old man said, "No, I'm not! I'm not dead. Can't be dead. Won't believe I'm dead until somebody proves it. Now, go away!"

Pretty soon, everybody in the village was there. Couldn't believe what they saw. The dogs howled at the scent of death, and the buzzards and crows flew overhead, lickin' their chops.

This went on for days. The stench got pretty bad. And folks got scared, especially when the old man started to turn grey and fall apart. But, no matter what anybody did or said, the old man wouldn't believe he was dead.

Finally, the doctor asked, "Sir, how can we prove to you that you are dead and should be gone?"

The old man seemed to study on that for a while. He scratched at his chin, and the skin fell off like dandruff. Finally, "Give me a funeral." said the old man.

"You had a funeral," said the preacher. "I preached it myself."

"Well, I didn't hear it," said the old man. "Give me another one. And this time, get me some nicer clothes to wear. And if I'm dead, I should have a marker on my grave to prove it."

Folks got to scurryin' about, got that man's best Sunday suit, and they polished his shoes and pressed his best white shirt. They combed his dead, fallin' out hair, they even brushed his ol' dead, rotten teeth. They tried their best not to make any more skin fall off, but it wasn't easy. They even slapped some wintergreen shavin' cream on that old man when they shaved his bristly whiskers, so he'd smell a bit better.

The village put its money together and paid for a wooden grave-marker with letters burned into the wood, letters that spelled out the old man's name, his date of birth and death, and the words, in big letters,

DEAD AND GONE. REST IN PEACE.

The old man sat in his coffin durin' the funeral, sat there lookin' at that marker, while the preacher preached and the neighbors mournfully sang and prayed. Again.

"Well," said the old man, "That was a fine funeral. And this piece of wood says, 'Dead and Gone,' so I guess I am." And he lay back in that coffin, and closed the lid, and was still.

Folks waited three days before they put any dirt over that coffin, had the doctor check every mornin' to make sure the old man was rottin' out, had the preacher preach every evenin', to send that old man on to Glory, or to wherever he was supposed to go. They wanted to make sure that old man didn't come back again.

He didn't. His days were over.

Now, is the story over? Well, unless that old man comes back, I guess it is.

Story Notes

A similar story can be found in *The Doctor to the Dead* by John Bennett, which was first published in 1946 (Rinehart and Company, NY). I didn't know that until someone told me they'd heard the story. My first thought was, that's impossible—someone in my daddy's family made it up. Maybe they didn't.

John Bennett collected the story and published it as "Daid Aaron II," stating that the story was told by Epsie Meggett and Sarah Rutledge, in Gullah dialect, in South Carolina; Bennett collected stories from those of African heritage along the coastal region in much the same manner that Joel Chandler Harris collected his versions of "Brer Rabbit" tales.

Daddy said he'd first heard the story in Tennessee when he was a boy. I have no doubt that the story brought him back to his childhood as he told it. His storytelling would take on a twang and grammatical format that seemed to preserve his memories of the tales, and that's how I remember them, with –ing endings shortened to –in', and colorful descriptive phrases that brought the dead, and the story, to life for me.

Jack and
The Old Woman

Once there was a boy named Jack. He lived with his mama on a little farm.

Every day, Jack's mama took care of all the work on that farm. She milked the cows and fed the chickens and tended the pigs. She swept the floors and dusted the furniture, washed the clothes and fixed and mended and tidied things. And that was before her morning coffee.

And what did Jack do to help?

Not a thing. Jack slept in until the sun was noonday high, if he was at home from the night before. He took his time getting up, and he waited for supper to be done and on the table. Then Jack ate his fill, and left for the night. What he did with his friends all night long, his mama didn't even want to know.

Every evening at the supper table, Jack's mama told him, "Jack, you need to help me around this farm. I've kept it up all these years just for you. And now, I'm gettin' too old for all this work, and I can't afford to hire anyone to help. If the work doesn't get done, if the crops aren't planted and the animals and the fields aren't tended, and the harvest brought in when it's time, we'll lose this farm.

"Jack, you have to help me. You have to work!"

Well, "work" was the word that sent Jack out the door. He'd throw down his napkin, and storm out of the house, spend his night having a good time with his friends. He'd come home as the sun was just beginning to blush at the very edge of the horizon. Sometimes he came home after the rooster crowed. But he always came home, and he never did anything to help his mama.

One evening, as the sun put himself to bed and the clouds rolled in from the southwest, Jack got himself dressed and sat down at the table for supper. His mama hadn't seen him all day, and she let him know it.

"Jack," she said, "I've said my piece on many a night, but you just don't listen. And I've tried not to say it, but I have to say it now. Jack, you are lazy. And maybe I should've said that before now, maybe I should've made you work more, and learn to work hard.

"But I'm tellin' you right now, things are gonna change around here. Tomorrow, come sunrise, whether you've had a good night's sleep or not, you are gonna get up when I get up and you are gonna work!"

Jack threw down his napkin, and headed for the door, like he always did. But this time, he turned to his Mama, and he fussed, "Mama, I'm tired of you tellin' me what to do. When I walk out this time, I'm not comin' back.

"I'm gonna find me a place where somebody will tend to me and take care of me, some place where I'll never have to work!"

Jack stormed out of his mama's warm, safe house. He walked as quickly as he could, with his eyes glaring straight ahead on the road. Black clouds quickly swept the evening away; the cold clouds opened up, first spreading a chilling mist, then spilling a freezing downpour.

Jack was too stubborn and too foolish to turn around and go home. He stepped into the woods to get out of the rain. Lightning flashed above the trees, and thunder shook the ground. The woods were no shelter from the rain.

Soon, Jack was sopping wet and chilled to the bone. He'd walked out on the warmth of his mama's home and the food she'd set on the table. Now, he wished for a roof over his head, a warming fire, and a plate of steaming hot supper.

Then Jack smelled something good, the aroma of wood burning. He saw a little cabin, its door open, smoke rising from the chimney, and warm candlelight beaming from every window.

Jack ran into the cabin. Inside, a fire was stoked high, its wood cheerfully crackling and sparking in the fireplace. In front of the fireplace was a rocking chair, with a wood box beside it. In the chair sat an old woman.

She didn't look at Jack. The rocking chair faced the door, not the fireplace. Jack figured the old woman had seen him run into her home. But the old woman's eyes were closed

She didn't seem alarmed at the sound of a stranger running into her house. She sat there smiling and rocking back and forth, back and forth, back and forth.

"Excuse me, ma'am," Jack sputtered, as he shook the water from his hair. "I just wanted to get in out of the storm, and I saw your door open, and…"

"Oh, that's alright, Jack," said the old woman. "Come on in. Warm yourself by the fire."

Jack didn't even worry about how the old woman knew his name. He trotted over to that fire, and wrung out his shirttails as best he could. "Thank you, ma'am," Jack said, as he warmed his hands by the fire.

The old woman sat with her eyes closed, and rocked back and forth, back and forth, back and forth.

"Are you hungry, Jack? I'll bet you're hungry. Feed yourself. The table is set," said the old woman.

Jack noticed a long table, set for one, and laden with all his favorite foods: ham hocks and collard greens, black-eyed peas and rice, corn bread and mulled cider, and sweet potato pie. Jack's mouth watered. "Thank you, ma'am," he said, and he walked over to that table, and started to eat.

"Feed yourself, Jack," said the old woman. "You can stay here, if you'd like. I will keep you safe and warm. I will keep you as my son. Would you like that, Jack?"

"Yes, ma'am!" Jack said. And the old woman rocked back and forth, back and forth, back and forth.

Jack ate until he could eat no more. And, you know how it is when your belly is full. Jack stretched, and yawned, and looked around the cabin for a place to rest. He could see no bed.

"Ma'am," he said, "Where will I sleep tonight?"

The old woman smiled, but she never opened her eyes. "Oh, you'll have no need for sleep, dear Jack," she said. But I will keep you safe and warm. You'll stay with me. You'll be my son."

The old woman waved her hand, and Jack felt himself stand up from the table, and glide closer to the woman, without ever moving his feet. He couldn't stop himself. He couldn't speak.

And the old woman rocked back and forth, back and forth, back and forth.

"Jack," she said, "my dear new son. Give me your clothes."

Jack's clothes flew from his body to the old woman's hand. She carefully folded the clothes, and the box beside her opened. The old woman placed Jack's clothes in the box.

Then the old woman rocked back and forth, back and forth, back and forth.

"Jack," she said, "my dear new son. Give me your boots."

Jack's boots slipped off his feet without him raising either one of them. The boots flew to the old woman's hand. She caught them, and put them in the box.

Then the old woman rocked back and forth, back and forth, back and forth.

"Jack," she said, "my dear new son. Give me your skin."

Jack's skin and his hair peeled away from his body. The whole thing flew to the old woman's hand. She gently rolled Jack's skin, and placed it in the box.

Then the old woman rocked back and forth, back and forth, back and forth.

"Jack," she said, "my dear new son. Give me your flesh."

The muscle and sinew and meat of Jack tore itself from his skeleton, and flew to the old woman's hand. She twisted it up, squeezed it dry, balled it all up, and placed it in the box.

Then the old woman rocked back and forth, back and forth, back and forth.

"Jack," she said, "my dear new son. Give me your bones."

Jack's bones glided close to the woman, close enough for her to touch them lovingly. She twisted Jack's skull from his body, and cracked and broke all the bones, so that they folded neatly, and she placed them in the box. The box closed.

"Ah, Jack, my dear new son," the old woman said, "my own son left me long ago, left me here , sick and alone, to die.

"But now, you are here, Jack. And you will be my son. I will keep you safe and warm, and you will stay with me forever."

The old woman rocked back and forth, back and forth, back and forth. Her eyelids finally opened. But there were no eyes behind them, only the empty sockets where eyes had once been.

The old woman withered, and shriveled, and faded, until all that was left was a wisp of blue smoke, that drifted toward the fireplace, and up the chimney, into the now clear and starry sky.

The fire dwindled down to cinders and ashes. One by one, the candles burnt out. The woods, and the cabin, were silent, except for the sound of an old rocking chair that moved back and forth, back and forth, back and forth...

Story Notes

Yeah, he's Jack in the box. That never occurred to me until someone at the Texas Storytelling Festival in Denton, Texas brought it to my attention. I'd heard Daddy tell the tale when I was twelve or thirteen, but I'd never put that twisted concept together.

Tales of Jack and his mama, rooted primarily in the folk tales from Celtic origins, abound in the southern United States, and have been recorded in several anthologies (for example, *The Jack Tales: Folk Tales from the Southern Appalachians*, collected and retold by Richard Chase [originally published in 1943 by Houghton Mifflin Company], *Mountain Jack Tales* retold by Gail E. Haley [published in 1992 by Dutton Children's Books], and Donald Davis' *Jack and the Animals* [a 2005 publication of August House], to name a few). They have been related by such magical tellers as the late and much missed Ray Hicks, the great Donald Davis (a personal favorite of my husband, Bruce, and myself), and the irreplaceable and desperately missed Jackie Torrence.

But I never read or heard this story retold by any of these icons of the oral tradition. I heard the story as Halloween approached; it was told as a bedtime story by my favorite storyteller, my dad.

I was trying to put this tale back together from what I could remember of it, when I met a storyteller from California, Audrey Kopp. She knew of a similar story!

Audrey sent me a version with a much happier ending. It had been printed in a publication called "*Appleseed Quarterly*, the Canadian Journal of Storytelling", in May 1994, as an article by Norman Perrin. Perrin said he had heard the tale told by Celia Lottridge in Toronto. In that version, Jack puts himself back together and goes home.

Daddy left Jack in the box. I am grateful to Audrey for helping me find a beginning for the tale. As for the ending, I like Dad's version the best.

Zuri Killed Me

"Zuri" means beautiful. And she was that–beautiful, with azure eyes, red-golden hair, and a body that any man would desire. When Zuri heard that the widowed man who lived in the cabin on the hill with his teenage son and his young daughter was the richest in the county, she made up her mind to get what he had.

What he had was not what she expected, land, and gardens, and a sturdy cabin, but very little money. He still worked in the mines, and so did his son. Like just about every other man in those hills and valleys, when they didn't work in the mines, they worked the land. In three days time, Zuri had moved herself into his house, with the promise of taking care of his little Lizbeth whenever he and Junior were gone. In three weeks, Zuri had moved into his bed, with the promise of becoming his wife. When he and Junior left, to work in the mines, Zuri went into town, taking Lizbeth and telling her to stay in the wagon. Lizbeth didn't obey; she saw the man and Zuri. She chattered about it like a little blue jay, all the way home.

You know how these stories go. Zuri killed Lizbeth. To dispose of the body, she made a stew, the meat cooked until it fell off the bones, the bones thrown out the kitchen window to settle in the stony earth. And when she heard her menfolk singing their homecoming songs, Zuri conveniently left open one bedroom window, then ran out to meet the men.

"Your little darling is already asleep. Come and eat before you go in to kiss her goodnight. I've made stew!"...But Zuri's father couldn't stand the smell of it. It smelled too sweet. Zuri's brother wouldn't touch it either. Zuri ate most of the pot.

Well, Lizbeth's daddy still wanted to tell his little girl goodnight. He left the table, and so did Lizbeth's big brother. Zuri was clearing her tableware, the spoon, the empty bowl, the napkin she'd used to dab at her mouth, when she heard shouts from Lizbeth's bedroom. The window! The child was gone. Perhaps something had come in and taken her away. Could it have been a man? Or, perhaps, a wild animal?

Father and Junior ran from the house and hunted in the darkness by the light of a lantern, but they couldn't find Lizbeth. Next morning, they went into town to form a search party; they promised to look until they found the child.

The men, young and old, walked solemnly from the house, and silently down the hill. And while Zuri washed her own breakfast dishes, she heard the squirrels scratching in the dirt and stones outside the kitchen window; the wind blew, smelling sweet, and in the wind, there was a song:

> Zuri killed me, stew she cooked me
> Brewed the meat away from my bones
> Here I lie, the squirrels a-scratchin'
> scratching here among the stones

Zuri stopped breathing for a little while. Then she went out and looked at those bones, licked clean and white, easy to see against the earth. Zuri picked every bone from the ground, wrapped them all in Lizbeth's dress. Then she got the shovel from the tool shed, and she buried the bones. That afternoon, as she hung the wash, the wind blew a bit harder, and she heard:

ZURI KILLED ME, STEW SHE COOKED ME
BREWED THE MEAT AWAY FROM MY BONES
HERE I LIE, THE STONES ABOVE ME
LYING HERE BENEATH THE STONES

Zuri ran for the shovel, dug up what she'd buried that morning, and buried those bones deeper. But before she could put the shovel away, the wind whirled and sang around her:

ZURI KILLED ME, STEW SHE COOKED ME
BREWED THE MEAT AWAY FROM MY BONES
HERE I LIE, THE EARTH ABOVE ME
LYING HERE BENEATH THE STONES

Zuri was frantic. She dug again, deeper, deeper. Zuri buried those bones again, and she transplanted a rose bush from the side of the house, planted it under the kitchen window, to hide her digging spot.

Zuri listened, listened, holding her breath. But the singing had stopped.

A year passed; Lizbeth was never found. The fields lay fallow, and any saved money was gone. Father and Junior, sick at heart, worked in the mines again. And Zuri packed, leaving to find someone with some real money. As she pulled a dress from the clothesline, she noticed the roses under the kitchen window. The rose bush had grown, with thick and thorny vines, and the roses bloomed blood-red and pungent with a sickening-sweet smell. A wind rattled the vines against the house; they clicked and clattered like dry bones, and Zuri heard:

ZURI KILLED ME, STEW SHE COOKED ME
BREWED THE MEAT AWAY FROM MY BONES
HERE I LIE, THE VINES ABOVE ME
RISING FROM BENEATH THE STONES

Zuri yelled, "Stop it! Stop it!" But the singing didn't stop. It seemed to get louder, the strange words swirling in the wind.

"If you won't stop, I'll stop you!" Zuri screamed. She ran to the barn and got the ax for wood-chopping; she rushed toward the vines, prepared to tear them apart. Maybe it was the hem of her dress that tripped her and made her drop the ax. Maybe it was the vines and the roots, rising up from the ground like fingers. Zuri fell into the bush. The thorns pierced her arms, her hands, her veins, her face, her throat. The vines, like strong arms themselves, held her in place as her blood poured down and sank into the earth.

Slowly, clothed in the buried dress, Lizbeth rose from the roots of the rosebush, and watched Zuri die.

When Father and Junior returned from the mines, it was to a tidy front garden and a well-lit cabin. Smoke rose from the chimney. On the front porch, as sweet and precious as she'd ever been, sat Lizbeth. Both men fell to their knees before the child; they hugged her, and cried. They asked her, again and again, "Lizbeth, where have you been? Where have you been?"

Lizbeth laughed. The sound was like music to their ears. "I don't know where I was," she said, "but I know where I am now. I'm home.

"Daddy, Brother, don't cry anymore," Lizbeth said. "C'mon! Let's go inside. Dinner's ready...

"I made stew."

Story Notes

I've always felt this was a horribly delicious and vengeful tale! Of course, it's a variant of "My Mother, She Killed Me, My Father, He Ate Me". In the story a wicked stepmother—wait. Why are these women always wicked in folk and fairy tales? Well, that's a variant of the true stories of fathers remarrying young women after their wives had died, in times from the ancient Greeks and Romans until today. In these old realities, the younger wife, a kind of "step-in" bride, was old enough to make demands on her husband's children and fortune, and often young enough to fool around with the oldest son, leading to soap operas that might end in murder. Such melodramatic situations simply had to lead to fictional tales.

The story was so ghastly that it fascinated me when I was a teenager and young adult. Without realizing I was "doing research", I started looking for other versions of the tale. From Northern England came a story called "The Rose Tree"; a girl-child is killed, cooked, and eaten, and the mother or stepmother–for mothers are sometimes wicked in these tales, too –dies for her treacherous act (S. Baring-Gould, "Household Tales," an appendix to *Notes on the Folk Lore of the Northern Counties of England and the Borders*, by William Henderson; London: Longmans, Green and Company, 1866). From Scotland came a tale of "Johnny", murdered and eaten, his bones eventually buried beneath some stones by his little sister. In both tales, a bird sings the song that leads the melodrama to its end, the stepmother's demise (Popular Rhymes of Scotland, by Robert Chambers; London and Edinburgh: W. & R. Chambers, 1870). In these versions of the story, good fortune comes to the surviving parent and other children in the family, but the murdered children don't return.

I think that's why I like my daddy's version the best. Lizbeth comes back, and gets even. Power to the innocent children, yeah!

Maybe those older tales were the root stories for my father's version of it, which I'm sure was something he heard as a boy. Daddy was born in Tennessee, as was his mother, Edna Maclin Cooper. His daddy, Louis H. Cooper, was born in Alabama. Both were descendants of African, Native American, and Scots-Irish Affrilachian heritage. Somewhere in that heritage rest the roots of this retelling. I gave the wicked protagonist the Swahili name "Zuri". It means "beautiful."

A Bedtime Story

Little Girl sat with her arms wrapped around her knees as she tapped her feet on the bare floor, in the cool, blue moonlight that washed through the dusty glass and Granny's sheer window curtains. She sat, anxiously waiting for Granny to come. Granny's old slippers whispered down the stairs; her old silk robe, the one Grandpa had given her, rustled, like a soft shower of rain falling around her ample body. She hummed, "Hush-a-by, don't you cry, go to sleep my little baby. When you wake, you shall have all the pretty little horses."

"Child," she said when she saw her granddaughter, "Child, why you sittin there? You know you should be asleep."

"Granny," Little Girl said, "You promised me some stories. I've been waiting and waiting. Tell me a story now, please, Granny?"

Granny sank into her rocking chair; it creaked as she settled herself into place, drenched in the cool-blue moonlight. She pulled her grandchild up and onto her lap, into her warm embrace. "What kind of story do you want tonight?" she asked.

"Oh, you know," Little Girl giggled and pressed her cheek against the smoothness of that silk robe. "Tell me a ghost story."

Granny sighed, "I'll tell you about the mermaid who came alongside your Uncle Joseph's fishing boat one evening. Your Uncle Joseph said the mermaid was beautiful, black skin shining as that sun went down, black hair like a bolt of silk spread out on the water, black scales like sparkling mica stone all along her fish's tail.

"The mermaid held out her arms to your Uncle Joseph, and she sang to him. Men said your uncle walked right off the deck, sank right down into the deep waters. Some of the men dove down as deep as they could.They tried to find him, but he was gone.The boat turned back to shore.The captain told me my son had leaned over the ship's railing to watch a seal, and fallen into the water.

"I knew better. I knew that, if you go back far enough along the branches and down the trunk of our family tree, well, some of the roots go right into the Caribbean Sea. I figured some pretty water mama had chosen your Uncle Joseph for a husband. I wasn't happy about it, but I wasn't worried. I just said a prayer and wished them well. But there was a funeral, without a body, and a memorial service beside the sea. I kept my head down so folks would think I was crying, but I wasn't. I was whispering to your uncle.

"I whispered,'Joseph,Joseph, if you can hear me, sometime soon, you come and show me your new wife.'

"Just before winter came, I was gathering up seaweed for my soups and my medicines, and I heard your Uncle Joseph call to me: "Mama, Mama."

"I looked out on the water, and there he was, your Uncle Joseph walking right up out of the waves. He wasn't even wet. He gave me the biggest hug. He said, 'Mama, I've left my wife. She don't want to do anything but sing and comb her hair all day. What kind of wife is that?' He told me all about that mermaid, how pretty she was, and how vain she was, and how he got tired of eating seaweed and snails, and how he had to learn how to breathe air again before he could come back on the land, how he bobbed in the water and took deep gulps of air and held them in his lungs so they'd know what to do—took him a while to get back to being a land-critter, but he did it.

"Well, he stayed home with me through the winter, stayed until the first buds of spring blooms, and started clearing my garden for planting. It shocked everybody that he was alive. But when summer came, your Uncle Joseph went off and joined the Navy, said the ocean was in his blood, and the salt air soothed his lungs. He disappeared on the water again. I never saw him after that. But every now and then, when I'm down on the beach, I think I hear Joseph call to me in the waves: "Mama, Mama." I never see him. I think, maybe he went back to that mermaid wife. Makes me wonder if I have some grandchildren with gills and fishy tails."

Granny laughed; she kept slowly rocking Little Girl, slowly rocking.

"No, Granny," Little Girl said. "Not that kind of story. That's not really a ghost story, and it's kind of mushy. I want a ghost story, please?"

Granny sighed, and said, "All right. I'll tell you about the old wild thing that lived under the ground in the roots of the apple tree…"

"Old wild thing was born one October night. Born howlin' and scratchin', tried to kill everybody. But the grandmother, she grabbed it, and held it tight to her, and prayed over it, while it screamed like something terrible and evil. It screamed and screamed, made folks eardrums burst, made their eyeballs bleed. Then it tore itself out of that prayin' woman's arms, run out and started diggin' into the earth, like it was goin back to where it belonged. The mother nearly died, and the father, well, he run off—everybody always said he was full of the devil. I expect that was true. And that grandmother, she planted an apple tree in the hole that thing dug, so's if it was still alive under the ground, it couldn't get back out. Apple tree grew strong and tall, but it grew sour green apples, too tart for cookin' or eatin'. Grandmother hung blue bottles all over it, tied 'em up there with red thread, to catch any evil that might rise up the trunk of that tree. But she didn't have to worry about that.

"Nothing from hell can touch an apple, nor the tree, nor its roots. Nothing from hell has liked apples since Eve offered the first one to Adam, and he ate it. You know the rest of how that story goes; what you probably don't know, was that once Eve and Adam had blessed that apple with the touch of their lips, apples been a blessing to humankind, and a curse to anything else.

"Why, once old Scratch himself came to my backdoor, and I nearly burned his devilish nose right off his face when I threw a hot apple pie—"

"That's not a ghost story!" Little Girl fussed. "That's a silly story. That story about that old wild thing just makes me laugh. I don't want to laugh, Granny! I want to feel all creepy and goosebumpy, all shivery inside."

"Fine," Granny said, "I'll tell you a sad, shivery tale, about a family that got sick, a long time ago. They caught a terrible sickness in the days after a terrible flood, one that destroyed most of the homes from here to the edge of the ocean. No one came to help them; pretty soon, there was no one healthy enough or near enough to help. The food ran out, then the firewood, then the hope. No fresh water nearby. One died, then another, and another,…"

Granny stopped her rocking. "Enough stories," she said. "It's time for you to sleep. I'm not in a mood for your kind of stories. I'll tell you one next time we're both awake this late." She gently pulled Little Girl from her lap, stood, and took her grandchild's hand.

"But, Granny, I really, really wanted a ghost story tonight," Little Girl pouted. Granny just walked, hand in hand with Little Girl, to the hall, toward the door, and through it, without it ever being opened.

Granny walked, her slippered feet silent, as were Little Girl's, neither one making a sound, neither one leaving a footprint, neither
one touching the ground. Granny's silk robe rippled and shone like
dull silver in the cool-blue moonlight, the moonlight that washed
through both her and her grandchild, as if they were glass and sheer
window curtain. The moonlight lit their path as they glided back
toward the cemetery, and sleep.

"Child." Granny's voice was as soft as the breeze that eased them
toward the cemetery's gates. "Child, you don't need a ghost story,"
Granny said. "You and I, we, are a ghost story.

"Hush-a-by, don't you cry, go to sleep, my little baby…"

Story Notes

This story is actually a combination of some family folklore and
superstitions from Grandma Edna Cooper and several women in
my Ma's family, and three stories I overheard as a child, listening to
grown folks telling tales on the back porch at my great-grandparents' house in East Liverpool, Ohio. They were told as vignettes, narratives that were not quite stories, shared in a conversational, "That's
not the way I heard it. This is the way that goes" manner. I wanted
to share them, but didn't know how. Then Hurricane Katrina devas-
tated the city of New Orleans in August, 2005, and I knew how to
stitch together this patchwork story, and how it would end.

I think it's also a good way to end this collection of Affrilachian
tales.

Acknowledgements

There are many who have helped me along the way to a story-telling "career". I especially thank:

Diane Ferlatte, J.J. Reneaux, and Dovie Thomason, who became my mentors as well as my big sisters in storytelling.

Bobby and Sherry Norfolk, whose support and advice gave me confidence for the journey into national and international storytell-ing.

My friends at the offices, on the board, and within the member-ship of the National Storytelling Network, for their willingness to share knowledge and wisdom.

Jimmy Neil Smith, Susan O'Connor, and Becky Brunson of the International Storytelling Center—Thanks for giving me the oppor-tunity to share my first national showcase at Exchange Place during the ISC National Storytelling Festival; over the years, it has opened many doors for me.

The many festivals that have invited me, and invited me again, to share stories with their savvy listeners.

Ted Parkhurst, my publisher and friend, and the giver of the go-for-it gumption I needed to get these stories and remembrances on paper;

The grand folks of Affrilachian storytelling who blessed, inspired, and supported me, especially

Mother Mary Carter Smith, born in Birmingham in Jefferson County, Alabama; Mother Mary now shares stories with the ances-tors.

Mama Linda Goss, born in Alcoa in Blount County, Tennessee;

Mother Mary and Mama Linda had the foresight and fortitude to imagine and create the National Association of Black Storytellers.

Finally, my deepest gratitude to Frank X. Walker, poet, educator, and wordsmith. Walker coined the term, "Affrilachian", in 1991; it became an entry in the New Oxford American Dictionary* in 2006.

*New Oxford American Dictionary, edited by Angus Stevenson and Christine A. Lindberg. Oxford University Press, 2010.

About the Author

Fourth-generation storyteller Lyn (Lynette) Ford was born in Mercer County in the Affrilachian/Appalachian region of Pennsylvania. Lyn shares from her family's multicultural Affrilachian oral traditions, in folktale adaptations and original stories she calls "Home-Fried Tales," seasoned with rhythm, rhyme, interaction, humor, and heart. Lyn is also an Ohio teaching artist in a state-based collaborative of the Kennedy Centre for the Arts, a story artist with the Greater Columbus Arts Council's Artists-in-Schools Program, a Thurber House mentor for young authors, a wife, a mother of grown and glorious children, and a proud grandma.

Lyn's works have been published in storytelling anthologies and award-winning CDs, magazines, and teachers' resources, including the Storytelling Resource Award-winning Literacy Development in the Storytelling Classroom (Libraries Unlimited).

The winner of a 2007 National Storytelling Network Oracle Award for Leadership and Service, Lyn shares her love of stories across the country, in residencies at schools and libraries, at conferences and festivals, "anywhere a tale can be told". Lyn has been a featured presenter at: the National Storytelling Network conferences; the National Storytelling Festival and the International Storytelling Center's Storyteller-in-Residence Program in Jonesborough, Tennessee; Tennessee's Haunting in the Hills Storytelling Festival; Hawaii's Talk Story Festival; the Timpanogos Storytelling Festival in Utah; the Mariposa Storytelling Festival in California; the Eugene Multicultural Storytelling Festival in Oregon, and the National Association of Black Storytellers Festival and Conference.

After her travels, Lyn goes home, takes off her shoes, and cooks the best oven-roasted ribs you ever tasted.

Index